A Revolutionary War Road Trip on NY Route 5

Spend a Revolutionary Day Along the Historic Mohawk Turnpike

Raymond C. Houghton

Cyber Haus
Delmar, NY

A Revolutionary War Road Trip on NY Route 5
Spend a Revolutionary Day Along the
Historic Mohawk Turnpike

Copyright © 2005 by Cyber Haus.
All rights reserved.

Revolutionary War Road Trips
are published by Cyber Haus
and printed on-demand
by Booksurge, LLC,
www.booksurge.com,
1-866-308-6235.

ISBN: 1-931373-21-3

Cyber Haus
159 Delaware Avenue, #145
Delmar, NY 12054
www.revolutionaryday.com
www.cyhaus.com
cyhaus@msn.com
518-478-9798

A Revolutionary War Road Trip on NY Route 5

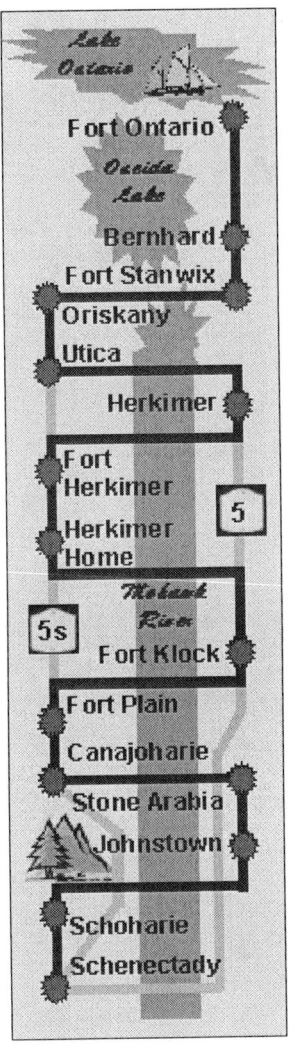

Spend a Revolutionary Day Along the Historic Mohawk Turnpike

OTHER REVOLUTIONARY WAR ROAD TRIPS
By Raymond C. Houghton

A Revolutionary War Road Trip on US Route 4
(Castleton, VT to Albany, NY, ISBN 1-931373-09-4)

A Revolutionary War Road Trip on US Route 7
(Pittsfield, MA to Burlington, VT, ISBN 1-931373-10-8)

A Revolutionary War Road Trip on US Route 9
(Kings Ferry to Saratoga Springs, NY, ISBN 1-931373-12-4)

A Revolutionary War Road Trip on US Route 9W
(New York City to Kingston, NY, ISBN 1-931373-11-6)

A Revolutionary War Road Trip on US Route 20
(Pittsfield to Boston, MA, ISBN 1-931373-19-1)

A Revolutionary War Road Trip on US Route 202
(Elk Neck, MD to Philadelphia, PA, ISBN 1-931373-13-2)

A Revolutionary War Cruise on the Champlain Canal
(Bethlehem, NY to Vergennes, VT, ISBN 1-931373-14-0)

A Revolutionary War Road Trip on US Route 60
(Charlottesville to Yorktown, VA, in preparation)

A Revolutionary War Road Trip on US Route 221
(Chesnee, SC to Augusta, GA, in preparation)

In memory of my mother
Phyllis I. Houghton,
who lived most of her life
along the pathways
of the Mohawk Indians

INTRODUCTION

New York Route 5 and its cousin, Route 5S, cross upstate New York and are collectively and historically referred to as the Mohawk Turnpike. They both parallel the New York Thruway (Interstate 90) and the Mohawk River. NY Route 5 hugs the northern bank of the river while NY Route 5S hugs the southern bank.

During the Revolutionary War, the battle to control the Mohawk Valley continued throughout the war from 1775 to 1783. Hostilities continued to occur even after the British surrender at Yorktown in 1781.

In Colonial times, the Mohawk River was part of a transportation route from Lake Ontario to the Hudson River in Albany. British control of this area would not only disrupt this transportation route but would play a role in a plan devised by British General John Burgoyne to divide the colonies.

In the spring of 1777, Burgoyne planned a three-pronged invasion along the Champlain, Mohawk and Hudson Valleys. This invasion would come from Canada in the north, New York City in the south and Lake Ontario in the west. The target for all three invasions was Albany, NY.

Unfortunately for Burgoyne, his invasion from the north

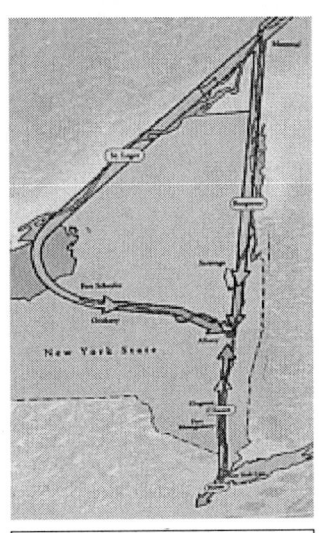

Burgoyne's Plan for 1777

(Fort Montgomery, NY Marker)

Revolutionary War Events Along Today's NY Route 5

1777
- Lt. Col. St. Leger lands at Fort Ontario
- St. Leger lays siege to Fort Stanwix
- Gen. Herkimer leads mission to relieve Fort Stanwix
- Battle of Oriskany
- Death of Gen. Herkimer
- Maj. Gen. Benedict Arnold leads mission to relieve Fort Stanwix
- St. Leger withdraws to Canada

1779
- Col. Van Schaick attacks Onondagas
- Gen. Sullivan and Gen. Clinton attack Indian frontier

1780
- Raid on Fort Plain
- The Great Raid of 1780

1781
- Americans evacuate Fort Stanwix
- Battle of Johnstown

1783
- Americans attempt attack on Fort Ontario
- Gen. Washington inspects central New York fortifications
- Treaty of Paris ends Revolutionary War

1796
- British evacuate Fort Ontario

was halted at Saratoga (Stillwater, NY) and the invasion from the south was abandoned after the burning of Kingston, about 50 miles south of Albany. The invasion from the west stalled at Fort Stanwix (Rome, NY).

A Revolutionary Day along the Historic Mohawk Turnpike parallels Burgoyne's invasion from the west. It begins early in the morning at Fort Ontario in Oswego, NY on Lake Ontario. This is where Lieutenant Colonel Barry St. Leger and his British forces would begin the invasion.

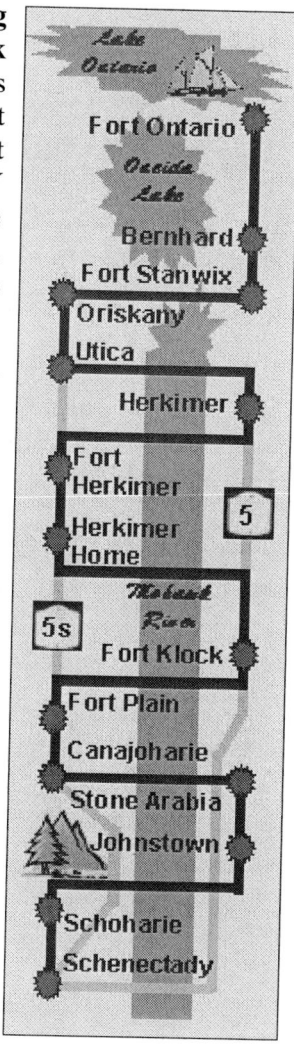

From Fort Ontario, the road trip heads south by Oneida Lake and through Bernhard on the way to Fort Stanwix in Rome, NY. This is where St. Leger's invasion would end.

From Fort Stanwix, the road trip continues south to the Oriskany Battlefield. This site was where General Nicholas Herkimer and his Tryon County Militia were ambushed on their way to relieve Fort Stanwix.

From the Oriskany Battlefield, the road trip turns east through Utica, Herkimer (Fort Dayton) and Fort Herkimer to the Herkimer Home, paralleling

the route taken by General Herkimer's militia to and from Oriskany.

From the Herkimer Home, the road trip continues east through Fort Klock, Fort Plain and Canajoharie and then detours north through Stone Arabia to Johnstown where Sir William Johnson would sew the seeds of support for the British cause among the Six Indian Nations.

From Johnstown, the road trip takes another detour — this time from the Mohawk Valley to the Schoharie Valley, which like the Mohawk Valley suffered the affects of many raids by British, Tory and Indian forces.

From Schoharie, the road trip turns east to rejoin the Mohawk Turnpike in Schenectady. During Colonial times, Schenectady was the head of navigation on the Mohawk River as rapids and waterfalls lie to the east where the Mohawk empties into the Hudson River.

TABLE OF CONTENTS
AND
TRIP LOG

Early Morning — *Mile Mark 0.0* ....Page 17

    <u>**Fort Ontario, Oswego, NY**</u>: The 1777 British invasion from Lake Ontario began here at Fort Ontario.

    Mile Mark 0.0 – 39.5..................................Page 28

    <u>**Oswego to Bernhard's Bay**</u>: Travel southeast, paralleling the route of the 1777 invasion.

    Mile Mark 39.5 ....Page 31

    <u>**Bernhard's Bay**</u>: The British passed by Bernhard on Oneida Lake three days after their invasion.

    Mile Mark 39.5 – 66.1................................Page 32

    <u>**Bernhard's Bay to Rome**</u>: Continue traveling southeast, paralleling the route of the 1777 invasion.

Mid Morning — *Mile Mark 66.1 – 66.3* ....Page 36

    <u>**Fort Stanwix, Rome, NY**</u>: Visit the restored Fort Stanwix where the British invasion ended after abandoning a siege on the fort and retreating back to Fort Ontario and Canada.

    Mile Mark 66.3 – 72.2................................Page 48

    <u>**Rome to the Oriskany Battlefield**</u>: Travel south to the site of the bloodiest battle of the Revolutionary War.

Late Morning — *Mile Mark 72.2* .... Page 49

> **Oriskany Battlefield**: Visit the battlefield where General Nicholas Herkimer and his militiamen (on a mission of relief for Fort Stanwix) were ambushed by British forces.
>
> *Mile Mark 72.2 – 81.6* .... Page 63
>
> **Oriskany Battlefield to Utica**: Travel east paralleling General Herkimer's route to Oriskany.
>
> *Mile Mark 81.6 – 87.6* .... Page 65
>
> **Utica**: Pass by the site of the former old Fort Schuyler where the wounded General Herkimer was put on a boat on the Mohawk River for his last journey home.
>
> *Mile Mark 87.6 – 103.2* .... Page 71
>
> **Utica to Herkimer**: Travel east along the Mohawk River past two of General Herkimer's campsites on his route to Oriskany.

Early Afternoon — *Mile Mark 103.2 – 103.7*. Page 75

> **Herkimer**: Visit the former location of Fort Dayton where General Herkimer formed-up the Tryon County Militia for their fateful march to Oriskany.
>
> *Mile Mark 103.7 – 106.1* .... Page 79
>
> **Herkimer to Fort Herkimer**: Cross the Mohawk River to the site of Fort Herkimer. After 1781, Forts Dayton and Herkimer became the furthest west strongholds in the Mohawk Valley.

Mile Mark 106.1 .... Page 80

Fort Herkimer: The wounded General Herkimer stayed overnight at the Fort Herkimer Church, the central defense of Fort Herkimer.

Mile Mark 106.1 – 113.9 .... Page 82

Fort Herkimer to the Herkimer Home: Travel east along Route 5S to the Herkimer Home.

Mile Mark 113.9 .... Page 83

The Herkimer Home: Visit the home where the wounded general would die while quietly reading his bible.

Mile Mark 113.9 – 127.4 .... Page 88

Herkimer Home to Fort Klock: Travel east into the heart of the Mohawk Valley, where British forces would stage many raids from Canada throughout the Revolutionary War.

Mid Afternoon — *Mile Mark 127.4* .... Page 92

Fort Klock: Visit the area where Patriot forces would stop one of the largest raids from Canada -- the Great Raid of 1780.

Mile Mark 127.4 – 132.7 .... Page 94

Fort Klock to Fort Plain: Travel east past the site of Fort Wagner to Fort Plain.

Mile Mark 132.7 .... Page 97

Fort Plain: Visit the site of the fort that was once headquarters to all the Patriot forces in the Mohawk Valley.

Mile Mark 132.7 – 137.0 .... Page 100

Fort Plain to Canajoharie: Travel east past the site of Fort Failing to Canajoharie.

Mile Mark 137.0 .... Page 102

Canajoharie: Visit the site where General James Clinton launched an attack to the southwest against the Iroquois Indians who had committed many atrocities in the New York and Pennsylvania frontiers.

Mile Mark 137.0 – 140.4 .... Page 103

Canajoharie to Stone Arabia: Detour north of the Mohawk Turnpike and pass the Stone Arabia Battlefield where Patriot forces attempted to halt the Great Raid of 1780.

Mile Mark 140.4 .... Page 105

Stone Arabia: Visit the sites of two of the oldest church congregations in the Mohawk Valley and the burial site of John Brown, the commander of the Patriot forces at the Battle of Stone Arabia.

Mile Mark 140.4 – 154.7 .... Page 108

Stone Arabia to Johnstown: Travel north past the area where Fort Paris once stood. When you reach the small town of Ephratah, head east to Johnstown.

Late Afternoon — *Mile Mark 154.7 – 159.2* Page 111

Johnstown, NY: Visit the home of Sir William Johnson, who built a Colonial empire here in the Mohawk Valley. His son, Sir John Johnson, led many of the raids from Canada into the Mohawk Valley.

Mile Mark 159.2 – 186.6..........................Page 123

Johnstown to Schoharie: Travel south back to the Mohawk Turnpike, cross the Mohawk River, and continue south to the Schoharie Valley.

Mile Mark 186.6 ....Page 129

Old Schoharie: Visit Schoharie's Old Stone Fort, which was one of the first sites attacked during the Great Raid of 1780.

Early Evening — *Mile Mark 186.6 – 209.8*...Page 137

Schoharie to Schenectady: Travel back to the Mohawk Trail in Schenectady.

Mile Mark 209.8 ....Page 139

Schenectady Stockade, Schenectady, NY: Take a walking tour of the Schenectady Stockade and the former Port of Schenectady, head of navigation on the Mohawk River.

Bibliography ....Page 153

About the Author ....Page 155

ACKNOWLEDGEMENTS

I would like to thank those who provided feedback and editing support on earlier formats of this book, especially my daughter, April Monica Houghton Blakeslee; my friend and mentor, Russ Denegar; and those who posted feedback on the Internet from the Mohawk Turnpike web site. I would also like to thank my wife, Jan Laws Houghton, for her loving support and encouragement.

FORT ONTARIO
OSWEGO, NEW YORK

The first fortification to be located on the site of the current Fort Ontario was built by the British in 1755. Called "The Fort of the Six Nations," or "Fort Ontario," it was destroyed by the French under the Marquis de Montcalm in August 1756, along with all other British defenses at Oswego.

Construction of a second British fort at this same location began in 1759. It was built according to the latest European military technology and designed to accommodate 500 men. It

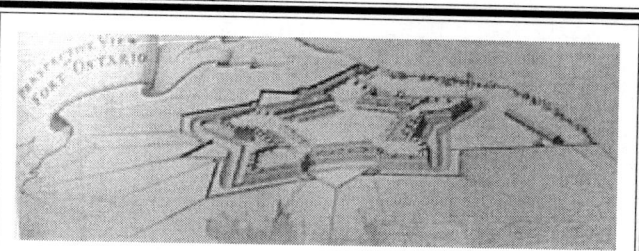

Perspective View of Fort Ontario

Lieutenant Francis Pfister, 1761

This second version of Fort Ontario was provided with positions for 46 artillery pieces and an initial garrison of 500 men. Reproduced by permission of the British Library.

(Fort Ontario Exhibit)

Fort Ontario

Built by English under Governor Shirley, 1755.

Captured and destroyed by French under Marquis of Montcalm, 1750.

Rebuilt by English under Lord Amherst, 1750.

Destroyed by Americans, 1778.

Rebuilt by English, 1782.

Surrendered by English and garrisoned by United States, 1796.

Captured and destroyed by English fleet under Admiral Yize, 1814.

Rebuilt of earth and timber by United States, 1839-1842.

Rebuilt of stone and concrete by United States, 1868-1870.

Post enlarged and built of brick by United States, 1903-1905.

This tablet erected by the Fort Oswego Chapter, Daughters of the American Revolution, July 4, 1906.

(Fort Ontario Marker)

contained a dry moat, extensive outer earthworks, and barracks. Small square or triangular forts called "redoubts" were located on strategic high ground several hundred meters away from the main fortification. The redoubts were built without rear walls so that if they were captured, they could be fired into by cannon from the main fort. The redoubts provided a formidable first line of defense for those defending Fort Ontario.

> "The present state of affairs in His Majesty's colonies, in which an unnatural rebellion has broke out ... precludes all immediate consideration in the domestic concerns of the Indians under your protection, nor it is to be expected that any measure which the King may think fit to take, for redressing the injuries they complain of respecting their lands, can, in the present moment, be attended with any effect. It will be proper, however, that you should assure them, in the strongest terms, of His Majesty's firm resolution to protect them and preserve them in all their rights; and it is more than ever necessary that you should exert the utmost vigilance to discover, whether any artifices, are used to engage them in the support of the rebellious proceedings..., to counteract such treachery, and to keep them in such a state of affection and attachment to the King, as that His Majesty may rely upon their assistance, in any case in which it may be necessary to require it."
>
> Earl of Dartmouth to Colonel Guy Johnson, Superintendent of Indian Affairs, July 5, 1775.
>
> (Fort Ontario Exhibit)

On July 25, 1777, Lieutenant Colonel Barry St. Leger landed at Fort Ontario. The next day, he would begin his invasion toward Albany with a British force of about 1,600 men, half of which were Indian allies and the other half were British regulars and Canadian volunteers.

At the end of August 1777, St. Leger returned in retreat to Fort Ontario with about half of the forces he left

**The American Revolution comes to Oswego
1775-1778**

The start of the American Revolution in 1775 sparked new activity at Oswego. The new British Superintendent of Indian Affairs, Guy Johnson, met with the chiefs of the Iroquois Indians at Fort Ontario to seek their support. He was only partially successful, as the Indian nations' loyalties were split between Great Britain and the American colonies.

After the British used Oswego as a route to invade New York in 1777, the Americans decided to assert military force at Fort Ontario. In August 1778, American troops burned the remains of the abandoned buildings inside the fort, but failed to destroy the ramparts or occupy it.

(Fort Ontario Exhibit)

with. This reduction in his forces was because the Indians had abandoned their ranks after hearing rumors that an overwhelming American force was sent to attack them.

After the failure of Burgoyne's three-pronged invasion in 1777, the British abandoned Fort Ontario. In 1778, the second Fort Ontario was destroyed by American troops based at Fort Stanwix. Despite the British

The American Revolution comes to Oswego
1775-1778

The start of the American Revolution in 1775 sparked new activity at Oswego. The new British Superintendent of Indian Affairs, Guy Johnson, met with the chiefs of the Iroquois Indians at Fort Ontario to seek their support. He was only partially successful, as the Indian nations' loyalties were split between Great Britain and the American colonies.

After the British used Oswego as a route to invade New York in 1777, the Americans decided to assert military force at Fort Ontario. In August 1778, American troops burned the remains of the abandoned buildings inside the fort, but failed to destroy the ramparts or occupy it.

(Fort Ontario Exhibit)

The British established themselves at Carleton Island at the source of the St. Lawrence River and from that post launched numerous campaigns via Oswego during the Revolutionary War. The major campaign took place in 1777 as part of a three-pronged attack on New York, whereby the British hoped to cut off New York from the rest of the American colonies. Lieutenant Colonel Barry St. Leger left Fort Ontario on July 26, but encountered unexpectedly stiff resistance at rebel-held Fort Stanwix. After a hard-fought battle near Oriskany on August 6, St. Leger retreated to Canada via Fort Ontario.

(Fort Ontario Exhibit)

After the unsuccessful attack on Fort Ontario, Lt. Alexander Thompson wrote to his brother on February 24, 1783:

"The day began to break which advanc'd so fast as to make it impossible to arrive at the work (fort) before broad day light — our guide confessed he was lost...The Orders we had from the commander in chief were positive, that if we did not attack before day, to return. Colonel Willet was under the Necessity of Ordering us to the right about — you may be assur'd we are sensibly mortified at the disappointment...We had two days a most severe storm and the whole of the time exceeding cold weather — we had three men perish before we could return to the lake — and we dare not make fire for fear of being discovered — we had one hundred and thirty bit with the frost, some very dangerously. I am myself one of the unfortunate."

(Fort Ontario Exhibit)

surrender at Yorktown, Virginia, which effectively ended the Revolutionary War, the British reoccupied Oswego in 1782 and rebuilt Fort Ontario for the third time. General George Washington ordered a surprise attack in February of 1783, but that failed due to the harsh upstate New York winters.

And despite the Treaty of Paris in 1783, which officially ended the Revolutionary War, the British continued to hold Fort Ontario. Finally in 1796, the fort

The British officer in charge of Fort Ontario at the end of the Revolutionary War took no chances that he would surrender the fort too soon. On May 14, 1783, he wrote to General Frederick Haldimand:

"I have received His Majesty's Proclamation of a general peace ... transmitted to me by a flag of truce from Colonel Willet, and a letter from that gentleman ... announcing ... a cessation of Arms on the part of the United States ... I have notwithstanding continued fortifying and all other duties ... until I am honored with your Excellency's directions."

(Fort Ontario Exhibit)

was turned over to the United States. After 1796, the fort would return to British hands during the war of 1812 and they abandoned it after the war.

Fort Ontario in the American Revolution 1778-1783

British regulars, Loyalists and Indians passed through Oswego on their way to raid Mohawk Valley settlements during the American Revolution. Recognizing the advantage an Oswego fort would give them if the Americans moved against Canada, the British rebuilt and regarrisoned Fort Ontario in 1782. As Loyalists fleeing to Canada took refuge at the fort, the British continued to launch scouting parties into the Mohawk Valley.

General George Washington viewed the fort's re-establishment as a sign that the British might invade New York again through the inland water passage. He ordered a surprise attack in February 1783 to capture Fort Ontario and seal off the route. That attack failed. When the war ended that year, Fort Ontario remained in British hands.

(Fort Ontario Exhibit)

In 1838, the United States regarrisoned Fort Ontario and rebuilt it over the next six years, resulting in the present-day fort. The fort became an Army Post in 1903 and by 1941, the post had grown to 125 buildings. During World War II, the fort was used as an emergency refugee center for victims of the Nazi

The United States gets Fort Ontario: 1783-1796

After the Revolutionary War, the British refused to evacuate Fort Ontario and six other military posts scattered from the head of Lake Champlain in New York to the Straits of Mackinac on Lake Michigan. They claimed the Americans had not complied with the Treaty of Paris in regard to pre-war debts and property confiscated from American Loyalists. The British presence at Oswego also protected the 7,000 American Loyalists who fled to Canada between 1783 and 1785.

The British prohibited Americans from settling in the vicinity of Fort Ontario and from moving goods through Oswego into the country's interior. They imposed high duties on cargoes shipped down the Oswego River to Canada. Hostilities escalated but were defused when the French Revolution diverted Great Britain's attention. The Jay Treaty of 1794 resolved the matter of the northwest posts. The United States took possession of Fort Ontario on July 15, 1796.

(Fort Ontario Exhibit)

Holocaust. In 1949, the site became a New York State Historic Site.

Post Cemetery — Along the lakeshore east of the fortification is the Post Cemetery. The cemetery contains graves of generations of soldiers and civilians who served or lived at Fort Ontario from the French and Indian War to World War II. Originally, the

"The American flag under a Federal salute was for the first time displayed from the citadel of this fort, at the hour of ten this morning. A Capt. Clark and Lieut. Pethergill, were his Majesty's officers left with a detachment of 30 men, for the protection of the works—from those gentlemen the greatest politeness and civility were displayed to us in adjusting the transfer. The buildings and gardens were left in the neatest order—the latter being considerably extensive in high culture, will be no small addition to the comfort of the American officers who succeed this summer."

Lieutenant F. Elmer
Fort Ontario

(Fort Ontario Exhibit)

cemetery was located about 300 meters to the south, but was moved by the US Army in 1903 to its present location over an old, filled-in quarry. Stone from the quarry was used to build the outer walls of the fort from 1863 to 1872. A blacksmith's shop, a stonecutter's workshop and a tool shed were once located around the quarry.

From 1944-1946, Fort Ontario served as a haven for 982 survivors of the European Holocaust.

Erected October 25, 1981 by Syracuse Pioneer Women/Na'amat and the Jewish Community of Central New York.

(Fort Ontario Marker)

OSWEGO TO BERNHARD'S BAY

Mile Mark 0.0 — Depart Fort Ontario using the south exit. Pass by the Art Association of Oswego on the left. Reach a stop sign at the intersection with East Schuyler Street. Turn right at the intersection.

Mile Mark 0.2 — Reach a traffic light at the intersection with Second Street. Turn left at the traffic light.

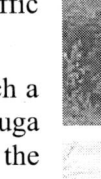

Mile Mark 0.3 — Reach a traffic light at East Cayuga Street. Turn right at the traffic light.

Mile Mark 0.4 — Reach another traffic light at First Street. Turn left at the traffic light.

Mile Mark 0.5 — As you approach the traffic light at Bridge Street, get into the middle lane. Go straight through the intersection heading south on Route 481.

Mile Mark 0.9 — Pass by Lock 7 on the Oswego Canal.

Mile Mark 8.4 — Watch for views of the Oswego River on the right.

Mile Mark 10.3 — Enter the city of Fulton.

Mile Mark 10.8 — Reach Mimi's Drive-in on the left. The classic drive-in is a great spot to catch a quick breakfast.

Mile Mark 11.7 — Go through several lights in Fulton and turn left on Route 3.

Mile Mark 15.1 — Pass through Volney Center.

Mile Mark 16.8 — Bear right onto Route 49 East. If you continue straight on Route 3, you'll end up in Mexico (New York, that is).

Mile Mark 19.1 — Reach a stop sign at the intersection with Route 264. Continue going straight on Route 49.

Mile Mark 27.0 — In Central Square, reach the intersection with US Route 11. Continue going straight on Route 49.

Mile Mark 28.2 — Go over Interstate 81.

Mile Mark 31.1 — Pass through West Munroe.

Mile Mark 35.3 — Watch for views of Oneida Lake on the right as you pass through Constantia.

Mile Mark 36.2 — On the right is a marker for the campsite of Colonel Gose Van Schaick.

At the campsite, about 550 Continental troops rested after attacking and destroy-

Frenchman's Island

Campsite of Van Schaick's expedition on return from attack on Onondaga, April 22, 1779.

State Education Department 1932

(Oneida Lake Marker)

ing Onondaga Castle, home of the Onondaga Indians. In the expedition approved by George Washington, Van Schaick destroyed 50 houses, killed 20 warriors, took 37 prisoners, and captured 100 guns. However, most of the Indians escaped into the woods.

The expedition was launched from Fort Schuyler. The British name for the fort was Fort Stanwix, an upcoming site on this road trip.

Mile Mark 39.0 — Enter Bernhard's Bay.

Mile Mark 39.5 — Watch for a small park that is on the right on the banks of Oneida Lake. This is a high-speed road so be careful pulling over.

Arrive in Bernhard's Bay.

BERNHARD'S BAY

From the small park sandwiched between Route 49 and the lake, be sure to note the view of the lake and the objects in the park, including the naval cannon, ship's bell and St. Leger marker.

Lieutenant Colonel St. Leger departed Fort Ontario on July 26, 1777. As indicated by the marker in this small park, St. Leger passed this spot three days later. To make his journey by water easier, St. Leger did not bring any large cannons. He would regret this decision upon reaching a well-fortified and strong Fort Stanwix.

> Over this Water Route St. Leger's Army passed to invest Fort Stanwix, July 29, 1777.
>
> State Education Department
>
> (Bernhard Marker)
>
>
>
> First settler near this spot John Bernhard made first settlement in Bernhard's Bay, 1795.
>
> (Bernhard Marker)

BERNHARD'S BAY TO ROME

Mile Mark 39.5 — Depart Bernhard. Be careful pulling out of the park area.

Mile Mark 41.8 — Pass through Cleveland.

Mile Mark 45.9 — Pass through Jewell.

Mile Mark 47.1 — Watch for the Marsden Marker and graveyard on right. Again, be careful if you slow-down or pull over to visit the cemetery.

As noted on the grave plaque, Marsden resigned from the British army and joined the American forces in Boston.

Mile Mark 48.8 — Pass through North Bay.

Mile Mark 49.8 — Reach the intersection with Route 13 to Sylvan Bay — a beach community on Oneida Lake. Continue going straight on Route 49.

Grave of Capt. Adj. George Marsden, staff officer of Gen. George Washington. See plaque at grave.

Oneida County D.P.W. 1968

(Bernhard Marker)

The graves of Captain and Adjutant George Marsden, personal friend and staff officer of General George Washington who died Nov. 12, 1817, aged 80 years. Also his wife, Wilmuth Lee of Virginia, sister of Richard Henry Lee, a signer of the Declaration of Independence, who died January 13, 1850, aged 93 years.

Capt. Marsden resigned his rank in the British Army of Occupation, then stationed in Massachusetts and accepted an office in the American Colonial Army at the outbreak of the Revolutionary War.

He fought at Bunker Hill and in all of the battles of Massachusetts and eastern New York. His conspicuous military brilliance won his promotion in 1779 to the office of Adjutant on Gen. Washington's Staff.

In 1782, Adj. Marsden married Miss Lee and located at Mystic, Mass, remaining there about one year. They moved to the then forest wilds of Bernhard's Bay and built their permanent home about 6 miles west of this plot. Their log cabin abode was honored in 1783 by a three-day visit by General Washington while on his tour of inspection of the central New York fortifications.

(Marsden Grave Marker)

Mile Mark 51.3 — Reach a traffic light in Vienna where Route 13 splits from Route 49. Continue going straight on Route 49.

Mile Mark 58.4 — Reach a traffic light at an intersection with Route 46 in Verona. Turn left and continue going east on Route 49.

Mile Mark 63.1 — Remnants of the old Erie Canal appear on the right as well as a restored Erie Canal Village.

Forty-one years after the signing of the Declaration of Independence, the construction of the Erie Canal began here on July 4, 1817. A little over two years later, the first section was completed from Rome to Utica. The

Erie Canal

Construction began here July 4, 1817. First boat trip from Rome to Utica, Oct. 22, 1819. 363-mile canal completed, Oct 20, 1825.

Oneida County D.P.W. 1969

(Erie Canal Marker)

entire canal, from Albany to Buffalo, some 360 miles, was completed in 1825.

Mile Mark 63.6 — Bear right at an upcoming intersection and stay on Route 49 heading east.

Mile Mark 65.8 — Get into the left lane as you approach a major intersection in Rome. The Fort Stanwix Visitor Center can be seen across the intersection. Turn left at the intersection and find a parking space for a visit to Fort Stanwix.

Mile Mark 66.1 — Arrive at Fort Stanwix. Dig out the quarters. Today, the fort is surrounded by parking meters.

FORT STANWIX
ROME, NEW YORK

The history of Rome as a water route linking the Great Lakes with the Atlantic Ocean is of historical and commercial importance. Except for the short portage across nearly level ground between the Mohawk River east of the city and Wood Creek to the west, a traveler in colonial times could journey by water all the way from New York City to Canada. Indians used the portage for centuries, calling it the *De-O-Wain-Sta*.

The Mohawk Valley in the Revolution

Fighting in the Mohawk Valley resembled a civil war within a larger conflict. Most of the Palatine (Rhineland) German settlers, resenting the lordly ways of Sir William Johnson's successors, lined up on the patriot side behind Nicholas Herkimer. Many of the Dutch-descended families had never fully forgiven Great Britain for seizing their colony in 1664 and eagerly joined the rebellion against British rule. But every ethnic group, and even individual families, were divided.

The old Dutch family of Schuylers were long-time rivals of the Johnsons, and it is not surprising that Philip Schuyler became one of the most prominent Patriot leaders of the Revolution.

From his handsome home still standing near Little Falls, General Nicholas Herkimer went off to lead the Tryon County militia in its march to relieve Fort Stanwix in August 1777, and here he was brought back to die from the wound he received in the resulting battle of Oriskany.

(Fort Stanwix Exhibit)

The Oneida Carrying Place

This path leading to the main gate of Fort Stanwix follows the route of the Great Oneida Carry where Indians portaged their canoes from the Mohawk River to Wood Creek. As the frontier moved west, traders and soldiers carried their canoes and long bateaux past here.

The carrying trail skirted swampy areas and followed high, solid ground. During dry seasons the lower landing were used and the carrying distance increased form 1 1/2 to as many as 6 miles.

The English guarded this strategic backdoor to the colonies with a series of forts, beginning with four small forts in 1756. Fort Stanwix, built two years later, was the largest. In 1777, American soldiers renovated Fort Stanwix and held it against a British invasion that threatened to cut the United American States in two.

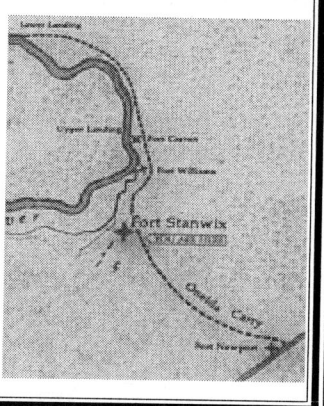

The shortest water route from the coast to the Great Lakes followed the Mohawk River to the Carrying Place where boats were portaged to Wood Creek. Lake Oneida and the Oswego River completed the route to Lake Ontario.

(Fort Stanwix Marker)

The English called it the Oneida Carry, and it became a funnel for commerce, settlement and military activity.

To protected this portage during the early years of the French and Indian War, the British built Fort Stanwix here in 1758 to replace three smaller forts. It was named for its builder, Brigadier General John Stanwix.

During the Revolutionary War, patriot leaders realized the need to defend the Mohawk Valley against British incursions and began rebuilding the fort in 1776. When Colonel Peter Gansevoort took command in the spring of 1777, there

were rumors of a British invasion from Canada down the Mohawk Valley by a small force under Lieutenant Colonel Barry St. Leger. Gansevoort doubled the efforts of his garrison, consisting of less than a thousand New York and Massachusetts infantry, to make the fort defensible.

Prior to his coming to bolster the defenses of the Mohawk Valley, Peter Gansevoort, the 28-year-old, Albany born commander of Fort Stanwix, had taken

Rebuilding the Fort (1776)

When the Revolutionary War began, Fort Stanwix was—if not beyond—the frontier. From his experience in Virginia,  George Washington had gained a keen appreciation of the importance of the frontier, and this may explain why he was determined to maintain an American presence at the isolated outpost.

In the Summer of 1776, at the request of Gen. Philip Schuyler, and earlier the Oneidas, the 3rd New Jersey Regiment, commanded by Col. Elias Dayton, occupied and began rebuilding Fort Stanwix.

Jonathan Dayton, the 16 year-old son of the Colonel, an ensign in the regiment, later was a signer of the Constitution and a U.S. Senator.

Another young officer in the 3rd N. J., Joseph Bloomfield, kept a diary of his experiences in the Mohawk Valley and went on to become a General in the War of 1812 and Governor of New Jersey.

(Fort Stanwix Exhibit)

> **The Mohawk River**
>
> Less than a mile from here the Mohawk River begins its eastward reach through the heart of New York State.
>
> Fort Dayton, 50 miles downstream, was the closest American settlement in 1777.
>
> The garrison at Fort Stanwix depended on the Mohawk River for receiving messages, supplies and reinforcements from the United American States. On the eve of the siege of 1777, while the main British force was approaching, the Americans were unloading a vital shipment of provisions at the riverbank. Just after the last load was carried safely into the fort, enemy soldiers appeared at the landing and around the fort.
>
> (Fort Stanwix Marker)

part in the 1775 invasion of Canada under General Richard Montgomery and, since March 1776, had been in charge of Fort George, New York.

Gansevoort's second in command was Lieutenant Colonel Marius Willett. Willett had spent most of his life before the war in New York City, where he  attended Kings College (now Columbia University) and became a wealthy merchant and landowner. During the French and Indian War, he took part in the Ticonderoga and Frontenac expeditions. Following the

start of the Revolution, he, like Gansevoort, participated in the 1775 Canadian invasion. The following year he was put in command of Constitution Island, a defensive position on the Hudson River opposite West Point. In 1777, he was transferred to Fort Stanwix.

By the end of July, Gansevoort and Willett had learned that the rumors of a British invasion were true. St. Leger's army of about 1,500 men was approaching Wood Creek, about 15 miles northwest of Fort Stanwix. Gansevoort was defending the fort with a force about half that of St. Leger's. The siege of Fort Stanwix officially began on August 3rd, 1777, after Gansevoort "rejected with disdain" the British demand for surrender.

Four days before the siege, General Nicholas Herkimer, having learned of the British Advance, ordered his Tryon County militia to muster at Fort Dayton near German Flatts on the Mohawk River

Water for the Garrison

The spring-fed stream reconstructed here supplied the garrison with water for drinking and washing. During the siege of 1777, the British caused it to go dry by diverting its source. However, wells dug inside the fort provided an alternate supply.

(Fort Stanwix Marker)

about 50 miles east of Fort Stanwix. On August 4th, Herkimer and some 900 men marched westward to reinforce Gansevoort but they never reached the fort. They were ambushed at Oriskany, an upcoming site on the road trip.

In the meantime, Gansevoort had sent a detachment of soldiers under Lt. Colonel Marinus Willett, to create a

British Artillery—Futile Thunder

British commander St. Leger ignored advice to bring larger guns, not expecting such solid walls and spirited defenders. The Fort's  commander later admitted that if St. Leger had brought "a few eighteen and twelve pounders, the Fort must inevitably have fallen."

"... at 11 o'clock this evening the enemy came near the fort called to our sentinels, telling them to come out again with fixed bayonets and they should give us satisfaction for yesterdays work, after which they fired four small cannon at the fort. We laughed at them heartily and they returned to rest."

from Colbrath's Journal
August 7, 1777

(Fort Stanwix Marker)

diversion on the militia's behalf. Coming upon British and Indian encampments, Willett's men carried away an assortment of kettles, clothing, muskets, spears, tomahawks, regimental colors and papers belonging to

The Raids

After 1777, the British never undertook a full-scale invasion of the Mohawk Valley, and no direct assaults were made on Fort Stanwix. Yet warfare in the valley became more fierce and destructive than before. Loyalists and their Iroquois allies, conducted devastating raids.

Congress and General Washington could not ignore these attacks on a valley that contained many staunch patriots whose rich farms helped supply the Continental cause. In 1779, one of the largest American offensives of the war was organized against the western Iroquois and placed under the command of Gen. John Sullivan of New Hampshire.

(Fort Stanwix Exhibit)

the British officers, including those belonging to St. Leger. From prisoners taken at the camp, Gansevoort learned for the first time of the battle at Oriskany and the size and strength of the enemy besieging Fort Stanwix.

General Philip Schuyler, commander of the Northern Department of the Continental Army, ordered Major General Benedict Arnold to take a small detachment from Saratoga west to the relief of Fort Stanwix. Rumors filtered into St. Leger's camp that the Americans were coming to Fort Stanwix in overwhelming numbers. In addition, coupled with the

> ### Pick and Shovel Assault
>
> Hoping to move their guns into closer range, the British began digging a siege trench. Zigzag angles protected the attackers from gunfire.
>
> Progress was slow, however, and only a few turns had been dug when rumors of an approaching relief force and Indian desertions prompted the British to retreat abruptly.
>
> The trench began across the street near the spot where the old brick City Hall now stands.
>
> (Fort Stanwix Marker)

deaths of several chiefs at Oriskany and the loss of their possessions after Willett's raid, the Indians chose to desert. St. Leger, finding Fort Stanwix more difficult to capture than he had expected and losing his Indian forces, was forced to lift the siege on August 22nd, 1777 and withdraw to Canada.

Lieutenant Colonel St. Leger, whose army besieged Fort Stanwix for nearly three weeks, called it "a respectable Fortress strongly garrisoned ... and

> Here August 3, 1777, the Stars & Stripes first flew in battle above the southwest bastion of Fort Stanwix (Schuler).
>
> Here August 2nd to 22nd, Col. Peter Gansevoort's New York & Massachusetts Continentals successfully withstood a siege by British regulars, Hessians, Mohawk Valley Tories & Indians under Lt. Col Barry St. Leger—Lt. Col. Marinus Willett Aug. 6th conducting the sortie to relieve the enemy pressure upon Gen. Nicholas Herkimer's Militia ambushed in Oriskany's Forest.
>
> 1758—Fort erected to protect the Great Oneida carrying place from the French.
>
> 1769—Famous boundary line treaty here negotiated.
>
> 1784—Treaty of peace with the Indians.
>
> (Fort Stanwix Marker)

demanding a train of artillery. We were not masters of its speedy subjection."

Fort Stanwix was garrisoned until 1781 but played no further active part in the war. In October 1784, American and Iroquois representatives met here to negotiate the Treaty of Fort Stanwix, which set terms

for a separate peace with the Indians and forced the Iroquois Confederacy (except the Oneida and Tuscarora tribes which had supported the Americans) to cede large parts of their lands to the United States.

Today, Fort Stanwix has been almost completely reconstructed to its 1777 appearance. In the course of excavations prior to reconstructing the fort, a substantial quantity of 18th-century artifacts were unearthed. These artifacts offered some evidence of the activities that took place here during various periods of the fort's occupation. Some of the building tools and hardware recovered from the site include picks, gate spikes, chisels, axes, strap hinges, nails, pintles, tomahawks, hammers and pipes.

Fort Stanwix is open daily from 9 a.m. to 5 p.m., April 1st to December 31st, except Thanksgiving and Christmas. During the summer, re-enactors can be found giving demonstrations in period dress.

ROME TO THE ORISKANY BATTLEFIELD

Mile Mark 66.3 — Depart Fort Stanwix and return to the intersection in front of the Visitor Center and turn left following Route 69 East. Be careful that you don't end up going under a bridge on the wrong route.

Mile Mark 66.8 — Cross today's Erie Canal.

Mile Mark 68.0 — Bear right and continue following Route 69 East to a stop sign. Turn left at the intersection and continue following Route 69 to the Oriskany Battlefield.

Mile Mark 72.0 — Arrive at the entrance to the Oriskany Battlefield. Turn left and enter the battlefield area.

Mile Mark 72.2 — Arrive at the Oriskany Battlefield.

ORISKANY BATTLEFIELD
ORISKANY, NEW YORK

The Tryon County Militia was a brigade of men between the ages of 16 and 60 commanded by General Nicholas Herkimer. The force was a part of the backbone of the New York State's defenses and could be assembled to meet any threat. Militiamen had to have their own muskets and equipment and had to train at least once a month.

In August 1777, 800 militiamen from the brigade went with General Herkimer to relieve the siege of Fort Stanwix. Supported by 60 allied Oneida warriors,

---

Historic New York
Site of the Battle of Oriskany, August 6, 1777

Oriskany Battlefield (Eight miles west of Utica)

The Battle of Oriskany was one of the bloodiest engagements of the American Revolution. British and Indians here ambushed the Tryon County militia as they were marching to the relief of Fort Stanwix (Rome). General Nicholas Herkimer, though wounded, rallied his forces and directed the fighting until the enemy fled.

Defeated at Oriskany and unable to force the surrender of Fort Stanwix, the British retreated to Canada. These reverses, with their defeat at Saratoga, thwarted Burgoyne's plan to divide the colonies by conquering New York.

(New York Thruway Marker)

Herkimer began the 40-mile march to Fort Stanwix on August 4th. Upcoming sites and markers on this road trip parallel Herkimer's fatal march.

Upon hearing of the march, St. Leger at the siege of Fort Stanwix sent Tory leaders Sir John Johnson and

---

Campaign of 1777

A three-pronged attack, known as the Campaign of 1777, was launched by the British under the direction of Major General John Burgoyne. The strategy was to split New England from the other colonies by gaining control of New York State.

During his march down the Mohawk Valley from Oswego to Albany, Lieutenant Colonel Barry St. Leger met unexpected resistance at Fort Stanwix, then under the command of Colonel Peter Gansevoort. St. Leger's small army of British regulars, loyalist Royal Greens and Indian allies laid siege to the fort.

Upon hearing of St. Leger's advance, Brigadier General Nicholas Herkimer assembled the Tryon County militia at Fort Dayton to go to Gansevoort's aid. On August 4, 1777, Herkimer, with 800 militiamen, began the forty-mile march west from Fort Dayton to Fort Stanwix.

When St. Leger learned that Herkimer and his relief expedition were on their way, he sent Joseph Brant, a Mohawk chief, with 400 Mohawk and Seneca, and Sir John Johnson, with 50 of his Royal Greens, to stop them. Their clash at the Battle of Oriskany was one of the key episodes of the Campaign of 1777.

(Oriskany Marker)

Joseph Brant, painted by Gilbert Stuart, reproduced courtesy of the New York State Historical Association, Cooperstown. Over 1,300 Iroquois listened to Guy Johnson's plea for help against the rebels. A number of Mohawks, led by Chief Joseph Brant (Thayendanegea), agreed  to follow Johnson to Canada when the conference closed on July 8, 1775. Brant also accompanied Johnson to London in March 1776 seeking fair treatment from the British for the Six Nations.

(Fort Ontario Exhibit)

The Military Road

Joseph Brant, familiar with the terrain, probably selected the place of ambush — where a small stream crossed the military road. The military road of 1777 was about ten rods north of the present highway.

(Oriskany Marker)

Col. John Butler to ambush Herkimer and his troops. Indians led by Mohawk chief Joseph Brant accompanied the loyalist supporters. They chose a boggy ravine two miles west of the Oriskany Creek as their point of ambush.

Herkimer had sent three scouts forward through the British lines at Fort Stanwix in an attempt to coordinate attacks with the fort. On the morning of the 6th, Herkimer's officers and men grew impatient and even mutinous while they waited for an attack signal from the fort. Herkimer pleaded with them but found

40-mile route taken by General Herkimer, August 3-6, 1777 for the relief of Fort Stanwix. The Battle of Oriskany, August 6, between Herkimer's men and St. Leger with his Indians was the turning point of the Revolution.

[Route]: Herkimer Homestead, Little Falls, Herkimer's Birthplace, Fort Herkimer, Fort Dayton (Herkimer), Camp - First Night, Turning Point to Great Ford, Ford - Turning Point to Fort Stanwix, Old Fort Schuyler (Utica), Whitestown, Camp - Night Before Battle, Oriska (Indian Village), Oriskany Battlefield, Fort Stanwix (Rome).

(40-Mile Route Marker)

restraint was useless. He ordered his troops to return to the march.

The Military Road and the Ravine

On August 6, 1777, the Tryon County militia marched down a wilderness road that entered this ravine. A "corduroy" road, made of logs, was the only means by which General Herkimer and his men could reach Fort Stanwix other than by boat.

The Military Road dipped more than fifty feet into this marshy ravine. A small stream, barely three-feet wide, meandered along the bottom. It was a splendid spot for an ambush. While 50 of Sir John Johnson's Royal Greens waited behind a rise, 400 Iroquois, led by the Mohawk chief Joseph Brant, concealed themselves on both sides of the ravine. It was into this trap that General Herkimer's militiamen advanced, with Herkimer at the head of the column.

Military Road, the path of the old military road.

Joseph Brant, portrait of Joseph Brant, by William Bercry. Reproduced courtesy of the National Gallery of Canada, Ottawa.

(Oriskany Marker)

Unsuspecting, the inexperienced and impatient militiamen marched blindly into the trap. As they crossed the swampy bottom and marched up the ravine side, the enemy closed in. Muskets fired from behind trees and Indian tomahawks flew.

The Ambush

Parched and exhausted from the heat and humidity on their march to Fort Stanwix, some of General Herkimer's men broke ranks and ran to this creek for water. Although Sir John Johnson had told his Indian allies not to attack until all of Herkimer's men had entered the ravine, they could not resist the opportunity.

As the militiamen laid down their muskets and placed their heads to the water, the Indians attacked. Tradition states that an hour into the battle, this creek ran red with blood. Thus the battle of Oriskany has also been called "the battle of bloody creek."

(Oriskany Marker)

In the first murderous volley, General Herkimer's horse was shot from beneath him and his leg shattered by a musketball. Sitting beneath a beech tree, propped against his saddle and smoking an old black pipe, Herkimer continued to direct the battle. In spite of heavy losses, the patriots fought bravely. Their stubborn resistance dismayed Johnson's troops. But the battle was so brutal that Brant's warriors abandoned the fight, forcing the British and Tories to withdraw as well.

Near this spot stood the Beech Tree, which during the Battle of Oriskany sheltered the wounded General Herkimer while he gave orders that made Saratoga possible and decided the fate of a nation.

Placed by Oriskany Chapter, Daughters of the American Revolution of Oriskany, and the Sons of Oriskany of New York City, June 14, 1912.

(40-Mile Route Marker)

The retreating British returned to Stanwix to find their nearby camp raided by a detachment of soldiers under Lieutenant Colonel Marinus Willett. The assault against Fort Stanwix  continued indecisively and when Brant and his warriors deserted, St. Leger was forced to abandon the siege and return to Canada.

At the Battle of Oriskany, nearly 500 were killed or wounded. The loss of so many able-bodied men was a catastrophic blow to the settlements of the Mohawk Valley. The battle, fought on August 6, 1777, has been described as the bloodiest battle of the American Revolution.

"I Will Face the Enemy!"

General Nicholas Herkimer, wounded early in the battle, was carried to a safer spot beneath a beech tree now marked by a stone monument. Although urged by his militiamen to retire from danger, he replied: "I will face the enemy!"

Directing the battle while leaning against his saddle and smoking his old black pipe, Herkimer noticed that the Indians were watching the white puffs of smoke from the militiamen's muskets. The Indians knew that in the few seconds it would take to reload, they could rush in to attack with their tomahawks.

After a violent thunderstorm caused a one-hour lull in the battle, Herkimer had his men regroup on higher ground. This time they would fight by twos, so that while one reloaded the other fired. This strategy quickly discouraged the Indians, who soon retreated from the battlefield.

Herkimer at the Battle, "General Herkimer at the Battle of Oriskany," by F. C. Yohn. Reproduced courtesy of Utica Public Library.

(Oriskany Marker)

A Final Attempt

Down this valley, the Indians, realizing the battle had been turned in favor of the Patriots, began to yell their cry of retreat: "Oonah, oonah!" Vanishing into the valley as quickly as they had appeared, they would carry terror to the settlements below.

After the Indians left, a detachment of Royal Greens decided to make one last try. They turned their coats inside out to disguise themselves to look like a relief party coming up the valley from Fort Stanwix. One Patriot soldier recognized the face of a Loyalist neighbor, however, and the battle raged once more.

Six hours after the battle began, both sides gradually withdrew. Although the Tryon County militia never made it to Fort Stanwix, the Iroquois losses at the Battle of Oriskany would lead them to withdraw their aid to St. Leger. Without enough artillery or other resources to continue the siege, St. Leger retreated to Canada, causing this prong of the Campaign of 1777 to collapse.

Royal Greens, Johnson's Royal Regiment. "The Royal Greens," consisted of men of the New York colony and Canada who remained loyal to King George III. Drawing reproduced by courtesy of the artist, Clyde Rixley.

(Oriskany Marker)

The battered patriots returned to their valley homes. Herkimer was taken by raft down the Mohawk River to his home where several days later, after an unskillful amputation of his leg, he died.

The Rally

Both sides regrouped during the driving rain. Herkimer's troops concentrated here, forming an irregular circle. The attackers were on all sides.

(Oriskany Marker)

For the first time in many generations, peace with the Indian nations allied under the Iroquois Confederacy was broken at the Battle of Oriskany.

Today, the battlefield is dominated by the 1884 Oriskany Monument. The 85-foot high monument was dedicated August 6, 1884. Its bronze plaques depict the battle and list the names of some of the men who fought at Oriskany.

"In the Valley homes was great mourning. For such a small population, the losses were almost overwhelming. In some families the many members were wiped out. It was many a long, weary year before the sorrow and suffering caused by the sacrifices at Oriskany had been forgotten in the Valley of the Mohawk."

Nelson Greene, *History of the Mohawk Valley.*

(Oriskany Marker)

To the Unknown Patriotic Soldiers of Tryon County

Who under the leadership of Colonel Ebenezer Cox, Colonel Jacob Klock, Colonel Peter Bellinger, Colonel Frederick Visscher followed Herkimer through the bloody Battle of Oriskany. And here on August 8, 1777 checked St. Leger's advance upon Albany administering the first defeat to the advancing columns of Burgoyne. Their patriotic sacrifices are commemorated by the Mohawk Valley Historic Association in the erection of this monument, August 8, 1928.

Erected by Oriskany Chapter Daughters of the American Revolution. A tribute to Colonel John W. Vrooman, who federated the counties of Oneida, Herkimer, Fulton, Montgomery, Schoharie and Schenectady into the Mohawk Valley Association which led through popular subscription to the purchase of these 48 acres and the erection of the memorial monument to the unknown dead of the Oriskany Battlefield.

(Oriskany Marker)

Also, on the grounds are several smaller monuments and markers. The Unknown Soldier monument east of the ravine was dedicated by the Daughters of the American Revolution in 1928. Two "40-Mile Route"

**Historic New York
Site of the Battle of Oriskany August 6, 1777**

The Battle of Oriskany was one of the bloodiest engagements of the American Revolution. British and Indians here ambushed the Tryon County militia as they were marching to the relief of Fort Stanwix (Rome). General Nicholas Herkimer, though wounded, rallied his forces and directed the fighting until the enemy fled.

Defeated at Oriskany and unable to force the surrender of Fort Stanwix, the British retreated to Canada. These reverses, with their defeat at Saratoga, thwarted Burgoyne's plan to divide the colonies by conquering New York.

Education Department, State of New York,
Department of Public Works.

(Oriskany Marker)

markers, which appear along the route taken by General Herkimer, are on the battlefield.

During its 150th anniversary in 1927, five acres of the battlefield, including the monument, were made a New York State historic site to serve as a memorial to those who fought so bravely and tenaciously to preserve their land and freedom. Additional acreage has been acquired through the years, and in 1963, the United States Department of the Interior, in recognition of the site's exceptional value in commemorating and illustrating the history of the United States, designated Oriskany Battlefield a National Historic Landmark.

The Oriskany Battle Monument

On August 6, 1877, the centennial commemorating the Battle of Oriskany was celebrated. Ex-Governor Horatio Seymour was the main speaker. At sunrise, salutes fired from the guns on the battlefield announced a glorious day. Every home in the village of Oriskany was decorated, and 70,000 people came to the celebration on foot, by wagon, horseback, carriage, boat and by rail. It was a day to remember!

Spurred on by the centennial festivities, funds for a monument were collected. This monument, erected from the stones of the dismantled Erie Canal weigh lock at Utica, was dedicated in 1884.

(Oriskany Marker)

ORISKANY BATTLEFIELD TO UTICA

Mile Mark 72.2 — Depart the Oriskany Battlefield and turn left on Route 69 heading east.

Mile Mark 75.0 — Reach the village of Oriskany. Watch for the naval exhibits and museum on the right.

Mile Mark 78.5 — Route 69 ends and becomes Route 5A, one of the many sub-routes of the Mohawk Turnpike. Head east on Route 5A toward Utica.

Mile Mark 80.8 — Route 5A ends as you reach the city of Utica. Follow the signs to downtown. Go under Interstate 790 and take Route 5S East into the city.

Route 5S, which lies on the south side of the Mohawk River, is another sub-route of the Old Mohawk Turnpike.

Mile Mark 81.6 — Reach the center of Utica at Genesee Street. Watch for the "Mohawk Country" marker on the left.

Arrive in Utica.

Aircraft Carrier USS Oriskany (CVA-34), 1956-1976.

(Oriskany Village Marker)

Historic New York
This is Mohawk Country

The majestic Mohawk Valley has been the scene of many key events, which have helped to shape the character and destiny of New York State and the nation. This was once the home of the proud Mohawks, one of the main tribes of the powerful six-nation Iroquois Confederacy. As the main gateway between the Adirondack Mountains and the Allegheny Plateau, the valley came to be used by French-Catholic missionaries, land-hungry settlers moving west, foreign travelers, French and Indian raiders, British Tories and American troops. During the French and Indian War and the American Revolution, it was a vital center of action — the main highway for east-west communication and a major point of contact between the contending armies.

The Erie Canal and New York Central Railroad followed the valley route and gave a new direction to its history. Internal improvements led to intensive settlement and industrial growth. While the valley has changed in many ways over the years, it still retains one element of the past — its incomparable beauty.

Education Department, State of New York, 1967, Department of Transportation

(Utica Marker)

UTICA
NEW YORK

George Washington Statue — A statue of George Washington at Valley Forge can be found in front of the Utica Public Library. General Washington visited Utica during a tour of the Mohawk Valley near the end of the Revolutionary War in July 1783.

To view the statue, turn right on Genesee Street from Route 5S. The statue is on the left about three quarters of a mile up Genesee Street.

Von Steuben Statue — After the Revolutionary War, General Friedrich Wilhelm von Steuben spent summers near Utica on land given to him in honor of his role as "drillmaster" at Valley Forge. He is buried on Starr Hill, 20 miles north of the city. Today, the area is the Steuben Memorial State Historic Site.

General Friedrich Wilhelm von Steuben was the person most responsible for the transformation of the Continental Army at Valley Forge into a winter-hardened, great fighting force. He was at onetime, a member of the elite General Staff of Frederick the

General George Washington at Valley Forge
(Utica Marker)

Great, king of Prussia. No longer in the Prussian army and without employment of any kind, von Steuben offered his military skills to the patriot cause. When he arrived at Valley Forge from France on February 23, 1778, he was armed with a letter of introduction from Benjamin Franklin. Washington saw great promise in the Prussian and almost immediately assigned him the duties of Acting Inspector General with the task of developing and carrying out an effective training program.

He formed a model company of 100 selected men and undertook its drill in person. The rapid progress of this company under von Steuben's skilled instruction set an example for the whole army. After training, the members of the company were distributed amongst the rest of the army to spread the training. This skilled Prussian drillmaster tirelessly drilled and scolded the regiments into an effective fighting force.

Major General Friedrich Wilhelm Baron von Steuben

Erected and presented to the city of Utica by the Utica German American Alliance, 1914.

(Utica Marker)

Slowly but steadily the endurance, bravery, and sacrifice of the soldiers at Valley Forge began to tell. Increasing amounts of supplies and equipment came into camp. New troops arrived. Spring brought word of the French alliance with its guarantees of military support. Now a strong, dependable force, well-trained and hopeful of success, emerged from the winter at Valley Forge.

The statue of Von Steuben can be found in Utica at the intersection of Genesee and Pleasant Street. The intersection is about a mile south of the George Washington statue on Genesee Street (83.4).

Old Fort Schuyler — In 1758, the British built a fort in the Utica area, one of a chain of defenses, which extended along the Oswego-Mohawk River water route during the French and India War. This fort was called Fort Schuyler in honor of Colonel Peter Schuyler, uncle of the Revolutionary War General, Philip Schuyler. The fort was abandoned in 1760.

1500 feet east of this spot was the Great Ford of the Mohawk, protected in 1758 by the erection of Old Fort Schuyler. General Herkimer used this ford August 5, 1777, on his march to the relief of Fort Stanwix.

Placed by Oneida Chapter, Daughters of the American Revolution of Utica, June 14, 1912.

(40-Mile Route Marker)

During the Revolutionary War, Fort Stanwix was renamed Fort Schuyler in honor of Philip Schuyler. The Utica fort then became known as Old Fort Schuyler. After the war, the name Fort Stanwix was returned to the fort in Rome.

After the Battle of Oriskany, the wounded General Herkimer was brought by litter to Old Fort Schuyler, where the American survivors made camp on August 6, 1777. Here, Herkimer and other wounded were put on boats and rowed down the Mohawk to Fort Herkimer, an upcoming site on this road trip.

To reach the site of Fort Schuyler from the Von Steuben statue, follow Pleasant Street for about a mile

---

Bagg's Tavern

Originally a log house founded 1794 by Moses Bagg. Washington, Lafayette, Henry Clay and General Grant were guests here.

State Education Department 1932

(Utica Marker)

The site of old Fort Schuyler, which though abandoned at the time, sheltered the wounded General Herkimer during the night of August 6, 1777, on his return journey after the battle of Oriskany.

Placed by the School Children of Utica, June 11, 1912.

(40-Mile Route Marker)

and a half and turn left on Mohawk Street at the statue of Christopher Columbus. Follow Mohawk Street for another mile and a half and turn left on Broad Street, heading west. After about two blocks, turn right on Second Street then left on Main Street. The site of Fort Schuyler is at the end of Main Street.

At the site, there are two 40-Mile Markers and a Bagg's Tavern Marker.

Lunch in Utica — A great spot for lunch, Lupino's Trackside Restaurant, is about a block east of the markers on Main Street. The restaurant, which is one of the "Town's Best," specializes in Italian fare.

Historic New York
Utica Area

Situated on the important Mohawk Valley route between the Hudson River and the Great Lakes. Utica has long been a travel crossroads. Indian trails converged there, and Fort Schuyler was built on the site in 1758. The community, which grew around the fort's ruins became the village of Utica in 1798.

During the American Revolution, patriot militia under General Nicholas Herkimer at Oriskany on August 6, 1777, halted an invasion by the British

(Continued on page 70)

(Continued from page 69)

compelling them to raise the siege of Fort Stanwix (Rome). Tories and Indians raided Mohawk Valley communities until 1781. With peace, land speculators reopened the area to settlement.

Governor De Witt Clinton at Rome in 1817 started the construction of the Erie Canal, completed in 1825. The Erie Canal, its Chenango branch to Binghamton (1836) and railroad service (1837) increased Utica's importance as a transportation center and the area prospered. Industrial production started early with textile mills along Sauquoit and Oriskany Creeks at Ilion. Eliphalet Remington pioneered in manufacturing firearms. Rome became famous for its iron, copper and brass works.

Makers of electrical and electronic equipment have replaced textile factories, while fertile farmlands continue to provide dairy products.

(New York Thruway Marker)

UTICA TO HERKIMER

Mile Mark 87.6 — Return to Broad Street and continue heading west. In the distance is Genesee Street, which is up on an elevated parkway. Watch for the ramp off of Broad Street that leads up to Genesee Street. Turn right onto the ramp and depart Utica on Genesee Street.

Mile Mark 88.5 — Cross the Mohawk River and go under Interstate 90. Watch for the directional signs to Route 5.

Mile Mark 89.0 — As directed, turn right at the intersection to Route 5.

Mile Mark 89.2 — Reach the intersection with Route 5 on the north side of the river. Route 5 is another sub-route of the Old Mohawk Turnpike. Turn right heading east.

Mile Mark 89.3 — Watch for the Herkimer Crossing marker on the left. Herkimer and his militia on their

At this point on August 5, 1777, General Herkimer with the greater part of his men and wagon train turned southerly to ford the Mohawk.

Placed by Colonel Marinus Willet Chapter, Daughters of the American Revolution, of Frankfort, June 14, 1912.

(40-Mile Route Marker)

way to relieve Fort Stanwix crossed the Mohawk ford near hear from the north bank to the south bank on August 5, 1777.

Mile Mark 91.3 — Enter the county of Herkimer, named in honor of General Herkimer.

Mile Mark 91.4 — Reach the town of Schuyler, named in honor of General Philip Schuyler.

Mile Mark 93.0 — Watch for the marker for Herkimer's Campsite on the right. Herkimer and his militia made camp here on the evening of August 4, 1777.

Mile Mark 94.1 — Cross over Interstate 90.

Mile Mark 94.8 — Pass Lock 19 on the right.

Mile Mark 97.1 — Watch for the Potash Marker on the left and the Fort Petersburgh marker on the right. At the beginning of the Revolutionary War, this area

General Herkimer camped near this spot on the night of August 4, 1777. With him were his 800 men and 400 ox-carts filled with supplies for the relief of Fort Stanwix.

Placed by Mohawk Valley Chapter, Daughters of the American Revolution, 1912.

(40-Mile Route Marker)

Potash Factory

Near this site in 1764, Peter Hasenclever built an ashery, which was the first frame building erected in the town of Schuyler.

(Schuyler Marker)

was the most western hamlet along the Mohawk River. The 30 or so log houses that were once here were abandoned by the civilian population during the war.

Mile Mark 98.3 — Reach the bridge to Frankfort. Continue going east on Route 5.

Mile Mark 100.3 — Reach the intersection to the town of Ilion (pronounced ill-lee-on, although it looks like

New Petersburgh Fort

A stockade built and used by the pioneers of Schuyler prior to and during the American Revolution.

(Schuyler Marker)

lion with two l's). Continue going straight into the town of Herkimer.

Mile Mark 101.6 — Turn left onto West German Street. Go under Interstate 90.

Mile Mark 102.5 — The road splits; bear left and stay on German Street.

Mile Mark 102.7 — Reach a stop sign at North Carolina Street. Continue going straight on West German Street.

Mile Mark 103.0 — Reach stop sign at North Main Street. Turn right and head south on North Main Street.

Mile Mark 103.2 — Reach downtown Herkimer at the Herkimer County Courthouse and Herkimer County Historical Society.

Herkimer County Historical Society Museum

Resource Center

HERKIMER
NEW YORK

In front of the Herkimer County Courthouse is a Fort Dayton marker, which was near this location. The construction of Fort Dayton was begun in 1776 for the defense of the Mohawk Valley.

In June 1777, news reached Fort Dayton of St. Leger's approach. On the 17th of June, General Herkimer called up the Tryon County Militia for field service. Just before he began his eventful march to Oriskany, he sent a small detachment of about 200 militiamen by river supply boats to Fort Stanwix to reinforce General Gansevoort. They managed

At Fort Dayton, near this site, General Nicholas Herkimer took command of the Tryon County Militia and on August 4, 1777 began the eventful march, which terminated in the Battle of Oriskany.

Placed by General Nicholas Herkimer Chapter, Daughters of the American Revolution of Herkimer, June 14, 1912.

(40-Mile Route Marker)

Reformed Church

This tablet is erected to commemorate the two hundredth anniversary, 1723-1923.

(Herkimer Marker)

to arrive just before St. Leger laid siege to the fort.

On August 4, 1777, General Herkimer formed up about 800 militiamen from his brigade as well as a long train of supplies destined for Fort Stanwix. They departed Fort Dayton for the fateful journey to Oriskany.

In mid-August, Major General Benedict Arnold arrived at Fort Dayton with a detachment of about 800 men from Saratoga for the relief of Fort Stanwix. While here at Fort Dayton, Arnold's attention was diverted by the mother of a convicted spy pleading for her son's life. He hatched a scheme where in return for his life,

Fred'ck Staring

Known as Frederick Starns on VA Frontier. Lost sons and grandsons in Revolutionary War 1777-80. Patriarch of old southern family Starn(e)s.

By Descendants 1998.

(Herkimer Marker)

> **Site of Early Village Burying Ground**
>
> Many graves were removed to Oak Hill Cemetery in 1897 to create Myers Park.
>
> Donor – Evelyn Dexter Arthur
>
> (Herkimer Marker)

her other son would carry information to the British forces besieging Fort Stanwix that a vast American army was coming up the valley for the relief of Fort Stanwix.

The scheme worked and Arnold returned to Saratoga to make a powerful contribution to the victory there — a victory that is called the turning point of the Revolutionary war.

Statue of General Nicolas Herkimer — A small park in Herkimer was the site of an early village burying ground. Today, it is a quiet park that contains the statue of General Herkimer.

> **Statue of General Nicolas Herkimer**
>
> Gift of Hon. Warner Miller. Placed on the boulder and presented to the Village of Herkimer by General Nicholas Herkimer Chapter D.A.R. in memory of those who have died for our country.
>
> (Herkimer Marker)

To get to the park, follow North Main Street about two blocks south. Opposite the Adirondack Bank is Park Avenue on the right, although it may be difficult to find a sign to confirm this. Turn right on Park Avenue and follow it about two blocks west to the park.

Fort Herkimer

Site of home of Johan Jost Herkimer, ca. 1740 fortified, 1756-57, military outpost during French & Indian and Revolutionary War.

Stone Arabia Battle
Chapter SAR

(East Herkimer Marker)

HERKIMER TO FORT HERKIMER

Mile Mark 103.7 — From the Herkimer Statue, go around the park and head south on North Bellinger Street until it reaches State Street.

Mile Mark 103.9 — Turn left on State Street and take the third right onto South Washington Street.

Mile Mark 104.8 — Cross the Mohawk River and come to a stop at Route 5S. Turn left, heading east.

Mile Mark 105.8 — Watch for the parking area with the Fort Herkimer marker on the left.

Mile Mark 106.1 — Reach the Fort Herkimer Church on the left.

Arrive at Fort Herkimer.

Near this spot was the site of Fort Herkimer, built in 1756, around the second stone house of Johan Jost Herkimer, father of General Nicholas Herkimer. Here Nicholas passed his boyhood and here he rested when returning wounded from the Battle of Oriskany.

Placed by Astenrogen Chapter, Daughters of the American Revolution of Little Falls, June 14, 1912.

(40-Mile Route Marker)

FORT HERKIMER
EAST HERKIMER, NEW YORK

Fort Herkimer Church formed the central defense of Fort Herkimer throughout the Revolutionary War. During the war, a swivel gun was mounted atop the church tower and a wall of logs surrounded the church.

After being wounded at the Battle of Oriskany, General Herkimer was brought to the church by boat from Old Fort Schuyler. He stayed overnight on August 6, 1777 and was moved to his home the next day.

A year after the battle of Oriskany, the Indian leader, Joseph Brant and a large party of Tories led a raid south of Fort Herkimer into the area that was called the German Flatts. A party of four American scouts came in contact with the raiders. Three were killed, but one scout, John Adam Helmer, was able to escape and warn the settlers in the area. All found shelter at Fort Dayton

Historic Fort Herkimer Church

1730 - 1753 - 1767

(East Herkimer Marker)

and Herkimer. There was no loss of life but much loss of property.

After 1781, Fort Stanwix was no longer garrisoned and Forts Dayton and Herkimer became the most western strongholds in the Mohawk Valley. In July 1782, another war party of almost 600 Tories and Indians raided the area south of the fort. Most of the settlers were able to find shelter and the raid was driven off.

In February 1783, in the dead of winter, Colonel Marinus Willett led the ill-fated attempt on Fort Ontario in Oswego from Fort Herkimer. The weather led to the failure of the expedition and the party of about 500 returned to the fort.

Later that year, in July, Colonel Willett greeted General George Washington at Fort Herkimer during a tour of the Mohawk Valley. Washington ordered that Fort Herkimer be set-up as a supply depot for the western forts, including Fort Detroit and Fort Niagara. These forts would eventually fall into American hands after the peace treaty with the British in 1783 after the war had ended.

Here was born Nicholas Herkimer, eldest son of Johan Jost Herkimer. He became a general in the Revolutionary War and the hero of Oriskany. The town and county of Herkimer were named in his honor.

Placed by Colonel William Feeter Chapter, Daughters of the American Revolution of Little Falls, June 14, 1912.

(40-Mile Route Marker)

FORT HERKIMER TO THE HERKIMER HOME

Mile Mark 106.1 — Depart Fort Herkimer.

Mile Mark 106.5 — Go over Interstate 90.

Mile Mark 107.8 — Go over Interstate 90 once again. Lock 18 is on left.

Mile Mark 110.2 — Reach the junction with Route 167; continue going straight on Route 5S East.

Mile Mark 111.5 — Pass the Treasure Mountain Diamond Mine on the left. Note the view of the Mohawk Valley below.

Mile Mark 113.3 — Reach an intersection with Route 169. Turn left on Route 169 and follow the signs to the Herkimer house.

Mile Mark 113.7 — Reach a stop sign. Continue going straight to the Herkimer Home.

Mile Mark 113.9 — Arrive at the Herkimer house.

Lieutenant Adam F. Helmer
Famous Mohawk Valley Scout

On August 6, 1777, carried military orders for General Nicholas Herkimer.

On September 16, 1778, warned the settlers of German Flats of the approach of Joseph Brant and his warriors.

Erected by the Mohawk Valley Historical Association and the Helmer Valley Association, MCMXXXVII.

(Herkimer Home Marker)

THE HERKIMER HOME
LITTLE FALLS, NEW YORK

General Herkimer's father, Johan Jost Herchheimer, was one of a number of refugees who, in 1725, settled at German Flatts. He was an industrious farmer who also engaged in trade and transport on the Mohawk River and held important contracts to provision the military garrison at Fort Ontario. As a major Mohawk Valley landowner, he acquired over 5,000 acres of land south of the Mohawk. It was here, about 1752, that his eldest son Nicholas established a farmstead.

Nicholas Herkimer pursued his own interests in farming and trade, which were particularly profitable during the French and Indian Wars. About 1764, he was able to replace his earlier dwelling with the English, Georgian-style mansion that today is the Herkimer Home.

To the memory of the men who passed along this route and fought with General Nicholas Herkimer on the battle field of Oriskany, August 6, 1777.

Placed by the Daughters of the American Revolution of Caughnawaga Chapter of Fonda, the St. Johnsville Chapter of St. Johnsville, and the Henderson Chapter of Jordanville, June 14, 1912.

(40-Mile Route Marker)

Historic New York
Herkimer Home ~ 1764

Three miles east of Little Falls on Route 5S.

General Nicholas Herkimer (1728-1777), one of the first American-born generation of the Palatine Germans who settled the Mohawk Valley, leading farmer-trader of the Valley, and hero of the Battle of Oriskany, built Herkimer Home in 1764.

As Brigadier General of the Tryon County Militia, Herkimer commanded the American forces who marched to the relief of Fort Stanwix (Rome) when the fort was besieged during the three-pronged British invasion of New York in 1777.

At Oriskany, August 6, 1777, British regulars and Indians ambushed Herkimer's troops. The General was wounded and died ten days later. He lies buried beside the homestead.

(New York Thruway Marker)

From this point General Nicholas Herchheimer, known as General Herkimer, started August 3, 1777, to take command of the men who assembled in answer to his call to fight in defense of the Mohawk Valley.

Placed by German-American Alliance of the State of New York, June 14, 1912.

(40-Mile Route Marker)

By the 1770s, Nicholas Herkimer had become the wealthiest and most prominent member of the Mohawk Valley's German-American community and  was active in local civil affairs. Herkimer gained military experience as a captain of militia during the French and Indian Wars. At the outbreak of the Revolution, firmly embracing the American cause, he was elected chairman of the Tryon County Committee of Safety and commissioned brigadier general, commander of the county's militia.

On August 7, 1777, after being wounded at the Battle of Oriskany, Herkimer was carried back to his home,

Herkimer Home

The legendary Revolutionary War hero, General Nicholas Herkimer died here, on August 17, 1777, of wounds received at the Battle of Oriskany. His grave and monument are in the family cemetery adjacent to the brick mansion built about 1764.

(Herkimer Home Marker)

where about ten days later his leg was unskillfully amputated. Reading the 38th Psalm from his Bible, he died calmly a few hours later. Herkimer's reputation as a hero of the American Revolution grew immediately, and today, his home is a shrine to the fallen hero.

The Herkimer Home was acquired by the State of New York in 1913. The Herkimer monument, 60 feet high, and the stonewall around the burial plot, were erected and dedicated in 1896. In the 1960's, a major

The Cemetery

After the Battle of Oriskany, the wounded General Herkimer returned home where he died on August 16 or 17, 1777. His grave remained unmarked until a simple tablet was erected by a family member in 1847. Other members of the Herkimer family and later occupants of the house are also buried here.

To prevent further deterioration from acid rain, in 1988 General Herkimer's gravestone was replaced by a cast synthetic reproduction. The original is on display in the Visitor Center.

(Herkimer Home Marker)

restoration was completed. The unspoiled landscape, including the Herkimer family burying ground, for the most part, remains unchanged from that of the eighteenth century.

The Herkimer Home site is open mid-May through October, Weds-Saturday from 10 AM to 5 PM and Sundays 1-5 PM. On Sunday afternoons, staff in period costume demonstrate household and farm activities.

HERKIMER HOME TO FORT KLOCK

Mile Mark 113.9 — Depart the Herkimer Home.

Mile Mark 114.3 — Reach the stop sign at the entrance to the Herkimer Home. Go straight across the intersections following the signs back to Route 5S East

Mile Mark 114.6 — Reach the intersection with Route 5S. Turn left, heading east.

Historic Indian Castle Church

1769, erected by Sir William Johnson.

(Church Marker)

> **Fort Hendrick**
> **1754-1760**
>
> British post guarding Mohawk Castle named for King Hendrick killed at Lake George, Sept 1755.
>
> NY State Historical Marker, 1929
>
> (Route 5S Marker)

Mile Mark 115.1 — Go under Interstate 90.

Mile Mark 117.1 — On the right is Indian Castle Church and marker.

In 1769, Sir William Johnson built the church on land owned by Joseph Brant, the warrior Mohawk chief.

During the war, the Indians tried to steal the bell of their old church, but in the process, they accidentally set the bell ringing. Alarmed patriots armed themselves, discovered the Indian plot and recovered the bell.

Mile Mark 120.4 — Pass Lock 16 on left.

Mile Mark 122.5 — Turn left on Sanders Road to St. Johnsville. Sanders Road is a small country road that goes straight down the mountainside to the Mohawk River.

Mile Mark 124.2 — Watch for the special breed of black and white cows on the right. Turn left onto River Road.

Mile Mark 124.9 — Turn right onto Bridge Street. Go under Interstate 90 and over the Mohawk River.

Mile Mark 125.6 — Reach the town of St. Johnsville and the intersection with the Mohawk Turnpike North.

St. Johnsville was founded in 1776 by Jacob Zimmerman, a Revolutionary War soldier.

Turn right and head east on Route 5.

Nellis Tavern

1741, Palatine settlement society.

(Route 5 Marker)

Joseph Brant
by Romney

Mile Mark 126.7 — Watch for the restored Nellis Tavern and marker on the right.

Mile Mark 127.4 — Watch for Fort Klock on the right.

Arrive at Fort Klock.

FORT KLOCK
ST. JOHNSVILLE, NEW YORK

Fort Klock was built in 1750 by Johannes Klock, a Palatine German. It was home to his sons, Jacob Klock, who was commanding officer of the Palatine Regiment of the Tryon County Militia during the Revolutionary War.

Three years after the Battle of Oriskany, Sir John Johnson and Joseph Brant led another one of their devastat-

Klock Fort

The Stone dwelling 500 feet south was built by Johannis Klock in 1750 and was used as a fort and place of refuge during the Revolutionary War. The "Battle of Klock's Field" was fought near here to the west.

This tablet placed Aug. 25, 1927 by the Klock Family Association in memory of the ancestors who toiled, served and sacrificed in this Mohawk Valley.

(Fort Klock Marker)

ing raids on the Mohawk Valley in October 1780. This raid is referred to as the Great Raid of 1780 because of the great destruction it caused and the many lives that were lost.

While area residents sought the shelter of Fort Klock, Johnson and Brant setup a line of battle between Fort Klock and St. Johnsville.

The American forces charged the enemy position and after a short skirmish, the raiders fled in an utter rout. Van Rensselaer's forces began to pursue the retreating enemy, but after Van Rensselaer called them back, most of the raiders escaped westward.

The Battle of Klock's Field was the end of the Great Raid of 1780. There are several upcoming sites on this Revolutionary War Road Trip that were affected by the Great Raid.

FORT KLOCK TO FORT PLAIN

Mile Mark 127.4 — Depart Fort Klock heading east on Route 5.

Mile Mark 128.9 — Pass the Palatine Church. Near the church is a camp marker.

After scattering the British forces under Johnson and Brant at Fort Klock, Van Rensselaer set-up camp here. He was later court-martialed in Albany for his failure to pursue the enemy but was acquitted of any charges.

Palatine Church Erected 1770

This tablet placed here by St Johnsville Chapter, Daughters of the American Revolution, August 18, 1910.

Erbauet imjahre Christi 1770 Den 18th Aug.

Palatine Church

Lutheran, founded 1749, erected 1770. The shrine of Lutheranism in the Mohawk Valley.

Army Camp

Of General Van Rensselaer's American Army, Oct. 19, 1780. Also site of Palatine Church, 1770.

NY State Historical Marker

(Palatine Church Markers)

Mile Mark 129.8 — Watch for the Fort Wagner marker and stone house on the left.

During the Revolution, this house was surrounded by logs to form a stockade. It became a neighborhood refuge during the Indian and Tory raids.

Mile Mark 131.2 — Enter the town of Nelliston.

Mile Mark 131.5 — Watch for traffic light at Route 80. Turn right and cross the Mohawk River following the sign to Fort Plain.

Mile Mark 131.9 — Go under Interstate 90 and watch for the sign to Route 5S and the Fort Pain Museum. Turn right at the sign on Willet Street.

Fort Wagner

Stone section of house was stockaded home of Lt. Col. Peter Wagner, Palatine Regt. Tryon County Militia, 1750.

NY State Historical Marker

(Mohawk Turnpike Marker)

Mile Mark 132.4 — Reach the intersection with Route 5S. Turn right and head west.

Mile Mark 132.7 — Watch for the markers for Fort Plain Museum on the left.

Arrive at Fort Plain.

1779 Clinton March

Colonel Lewis Dubois with 5th New York Regiment and artillery left Fort Plain for Otsego Lake, June 25, 1779.

NY State Historical Marker, 1928

(Route 5S Marker)

FORT PLAIN
NEW YORK

Fort Plain was built by Colonel Dayton of the Continental Army in 1776 on the site of today's Fort Plain Museum. Like other forts in the Mohawk Valley at the time, it was a refuge for neighbors during the savage raids by British forces that were comprised of Tories and Indians.

In one such raid, in August of 1780, women helped to "man" Fort Plain. After seeking refuge in the fort, the women donned men's hats and carried poles. Showing themselves sufficiently above the stockade, the Indians and Tories retreated after seeing what appeared to be a large garrison at the fort, ending their August Raid.

Later in 1780, General Robert Van Rensselaer made Fort Plain his headquarters, renaming Fort Plain after

Fort Plain Museum

Site of Revolutionary War fort and blockhouse. 1780-1783. National register historic site.

(Fort Plain Marker)

> **"Let the Work of our Fathers Stand"**
>
> On the adjacent hill summit stood Fort Plain erected 1776 and its blockhouse, built 1780. Military headquarters of the Mohawk Valley, 1780-1784. General Washington here July 30, 1783.
>
> Erected by Fort Plain Chapter Daughters of the American Revolution, October 19, 1928.
>
> (Fort Plain Marker)

himself, Fort Rensselaer; however, the name change did not stick.

In June 1781, Colonel Marinus Willett was given command of the forces in the Mohawk Valley and took up headquarters at Fort Plain. Willett, whose home was

> **FORT PLAIN**
> **1776-1786**
>
> Northern limit of raid by Brant's Indians — Tories: 16 killed - 60 captured. 100 buildings burned, August 2, 1780
>
> New York State historical marker.
>
> (Fort Plain Marker)

the British-occupied New York City, was well respected in the valley and was eventually promoted to general. Later, he became mayor of New York City.

On July 31, 1783, General George Washington inspected the garrison of Fort Plain and was given a military salute on his tour of the Mohawk Valley near the end of the war.

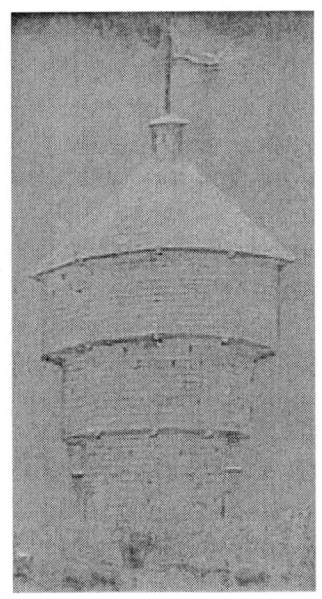

FORT PLAIN TO CANAJOHARIE

Mile Mark 132.7 — Depart the Fort Plain Museum heading east on Route 5S.

Mile Mark 133.6 — Reach downtown Fort Plain. Make the left at the light and the next right. Continue east on Route 5S.

Mile Mark 135.6 — Watch for the Fort Failing marker that is across the bike path, which at this point is part of ten lanes of traffic on the south side of the Mohawk River. The ten lanes include two for old Route 5S, two for the bike path, two for Route 5S and four for Interstate 90.

Mile Mark 136.2 — Watch for the speed zone warning marker and cross over to old Route 5S on the right and take the old road into Canajoharie.

Fort Failing

Home and place of refuge built ca. 1770, by Nicholas Failing for his son Henry, later the home of Colonel Hendrick Frey.

(Route 5S Marker)

Mile Mark 137.0 — Reach Canajoharie's signature low traffic light in the middle of a small roundabout in the center of town. Look for the markers on the right.

Arrive at Canajoharie.

Site of Johannes Reuff's Tavern

Built 1750 by Hendrick Schrembling. Became Reuff's Tavern in 1778. General James Clinton's Headquarters in 1779. General Washington visited here in 1783. Recruiting office 1812. Demolished 1850.

(Canajoharie Marker)

CANAJOHARIE
NEW YORK

In 1779, General George Washington could no longer ignore the attacks being committed by the Iroquois Indians along the New York and Pennsylvania frontiers. He ordered General John Sullivan and General James Clinton to lead an expedition against the Indians.

General James Clinton was directed to proceed up the Mohawk River from Schenectady to Canajoharie, head south to the southwestern corner of New York where he would meet General Sullivan, and continue the expedition into Pennsylvania.

Today, Route 10 South generally follows the route taken by Clinton on June 17, 1779. Under Clinton and Sullivan, the army decisively defeated the Indians and Tories at a battle near Elmira, NY. Later, they thoroughly destroyed the homes and the countryside of the Indian Six Nations.

This fountain marks the northeastern terminal of the Continental Road, constructed under the supervision of General Clinton, to Otsego Lake, June 17, 1779.

Erected by Fort Rensselaer Chapter, Daughters of the American Revolution, of Canajoharie, NY, June 17, 1911.

(Canajoharie Marker)

CANAJOHARIE TO STONE ARABIA

Mile Mark 137.0 — Depart Canajoharie. Proceed around the rotary and head north on Route 10 passing Canajoharie's main industry, Beech-Nut Foods.

Mile Mark 137.2 — Cross Route 5S and go under I90 and across the Mohawk River.

Mile Mark 137.4 — Turn left at the light in front of McDonalds and head west briefly on Route 5.

Mile Mark 137.5 — Detour right and continue heading north on Route 10. Keep a watchful eye for locals who,

Stone Arabia Battlefield

Lies east of road. Col. Brown's American Battalion defeated, Oct. 19, 1780.

NY State Historical Marker

(Route 10 Marker)

today, still travel this area by slow-moving horse and buggy.

Mile Mark 139.2 — Pass the Stone Arabia Battlefield on the right.

Before the battle at Klock's field, Colonel John Brown boldly attacked the advance guard of the British forces of the Great Raid of 1780 here in this open field. However, his battalion was quickly outnumbered and was soundly defeated. General Robert Van Rensselaer failed to reinforce his position and Colonel John Brown was killed in the battle.

Mile Mark 140.4 — Reach the Stone Arabia churches and the grave of John Brown.

STONE ARABIA
NEW YORK

Today, downtown Stone Arabia is comprised of two churches — a Lutheran Church and a Dutch Reformed Church. The congregations of these two churches are among the oldest in the Mohawk Valley. One cannot help but feel the spirit of these churches as one strolls amongst them and the cemeteries behind.

Trinity Lutheran Church

Site acquired, June 2, 1728. Log church built by Lutheran and reformed Palatines. A later church burned by Tories and Indians, 1780. Present building erected in 1792. Oldest Lutheran Congregation in the Mohawk Valley.

Erected by Church and State of NY, 1929.

(Stone Arabia Marker)

✠

Former reformed Dutch Church. Organized 1711. Built 1788. Listed on the National Register of Historic Places, 1977. Reformed Church services were held here until 1990.

Erected 1998.

(Stone Arabia Marker)

Both of the existing structures were built after the Revolutionary War. They replaced the churches that were destroyed during the Great Raid of 1780.

Colonel John Brown's grave lies behind the Dutch Reformed Church. A monument can be found over his grave.

Col. John Brown and other Revolutionary soldiers are buried west of this church.

This marker erected by Fort Rensselaer Chapter DAR, Canajoharie, NY, 1915.

(Stone Arabia Marker)

John Brown, whose home was Pittsfield, Massachusetts, helped to organize in Pittsfield the mission to take Fort Ticonderoga in 1775. He marched from Pittsfield to enlist Ethan Allen and the Green Mountain Boys into the expedition and participated with Ethan Allen in the capture of the fort. Many of the cannons acquired from the fort were moved to Boston where their use was largely responsible for the British retreat from Boston in 1776.

Fort Ticonderoga was taken back by the British during Burgoyne's 1777 invasion. Brown led another mission in the fall of 1777 to attempt to recapture the fort. However, this time Brown found the fort well fortified, and it held against the American attack.

STONE ARABIA TO JOHNSTOWN

Mile Mark 140.4 — Depart Stone Arabia heading north on Route 10.

Mile Mark 141.0 — Pass the area where Fort Paris once stood.

Sir John Johnson bypassed Fort Paris during the Great Raid of 1780 and went up the Mohawk Valley. Later, the timbers that once formed the fort were used to rebuild area structures destroyed during the raid.

Mile Mark 141.3 — Pass the Louck's Tavern marker.

Mile Mark 142.1 — Make the sharp turn to the right then the left at Logan Farms.

Mile Mark 144.1 — Route 67 joins Route 10.

Mile Mark 144.5 — Pass the Frederick Getman Marker on the right.

Mile Mark 145.1 — Reach the center of the town of Ephratah.

Louck's Tavern

Site of first meeting place, Palatine District Committee of Safety, August 27, 1774.

NY State Historical Marker

(Route 10 Marker)

> **Site of Home of Frederick Getman**
>
>
>
> Came to America in 1710. Naturalized on November 22, 1715. Purchased 600 acres of land in Stone Arabia Patent and settled here in 1720. His sons and descendants were prominent in early civil and military life in the colony and state.
>
> Erected by State Education Department and descendents of Frederick Getman, 1934.
>
> (Route 10 Marker)

Mile Mark 145.5 — Watch for the old Grist Mill marker on the right; it is just up a side street.

Mile Mark 145.8 — Turn right on Route 67 going east to Johnstown.

Mile Mark 153.0 — Reach the junction with Route 334. Continue going east on Route 67.

> **Old Grist Mill**
>
> Built 1770 by Sir William Johnson. Burned during a Revolutionary War Indian raid. One William Cool killed Ozias Krep made prisoner.
>
> Bicentennial Fulton Co. 1975
>
> (Route 10 Marker)

Mile Mark 154.7 — Reach the intersection with Route 29 and downtown Johnstown. Find a parking place for a walking tour around downtown Johnstown.

Arrive in Johnstown.

JOHNSTOWN
NEW YORK

In the 1760's, Johnstown was located at the intersection of six Indian trails. Sir William Johnson secured peace among the Indians and built a Colonial

---

The Mohawk Valley in the Revolution

The course of American history would have been much different had Sir William Johnson been alive when the Revolution began, but he died at an Indian conference in 1774. Even  collectively, his successors could not fill the void, though they did their utmost for the British Crown during the Revolution.

Sir William's son, Sir John inherited his title. In 1776, fearing an attack by the revolutionaries, he fled to Canada and organized a Loyalist regiment. He was with St. Leger in the attack on Fort Stanwix in 1777 and led a large-scale raid on the Valley in 1780.

Perhaps the most dreaded foe of the patriots was the Mohawk Joseph Brant. Cultured, religious and well educated, he remained an Indian patriot and fought tirelessly against the rebels. He felt that the Iroquois would have a better chance of preserving their way of life under British rule than under the land-hungry colonists.

(Fort Stanwix Exhibit)

empire here in the Mohawk Valley. He built a school, churches, forts, farms and a town.

Sir William Johnson died just a year before the beginning of the Revolutionary War. In January 1776, an American force of about 3,000 men under Philip Schuyler and Nicholas Herkimer disarmed his son, Sir

---

Historic New York
Mohawk Area

The Mohawk Valley was a principal pass to the interior between the Adirondack Mountains and the Allegheny Plateau. Here dwelt the Mohawks, one of the Nations of the Iroquois Confederacy who barred the white man's advance westward. In the seventeenth century they were visited by French Catholic missionaries from Canada, some of whom suffered martyrdom. In 1712, with the aid of Queen Anne, an Anglican Chapel for the Mohawks was erected at Fort Hunter.

Trade goods and furs were carried by riverboats over the Mohawk between Albany and the West. The same route was followed by military expeditions during the French and Indian War.

From Fort Johnson, and after 1763 from Johnson Hall at Johnstown, Sir William Johnson ably conducted Indian affairs for the British government. During the Revolution, Tory and Indian raiders from Canada harassed the Mohawk Valley settlements.

The completion of the Erie Canal in 1825 and the formation of the New York Central Railroad in 1853 introduced an era of rapid settlement and industrial growth. In the twentieth century improved highways follow this historic route, long famed for its beauty.

(New York Thruway Marker)

John Johnson and his followers. A few months later, fearing capture, they escaped into Canada.

In March 1778, Schuyler returned to Johnstown in an attempt to seek neutrality among the Indian tribes. The council with the Indians was, for the most part, unsuccessful because most of the tribes were already in alliance with the British.

In a prelude to the Great Raid of 1780, Sir John Johnson and his small army of Tories and Indians came back from Canada and invaded Johnstown on May 21, 1780. Their raid began at midnight when they entered the town and systematically killed local patriots and destroyed their homes and property. Local Tories, who had an early warning about the raid, assisted with the raid on their fellow neighbors. After Johnstown, the raiders continued their destruction south to the Mohawk River then returned to Canada with their captured booty.

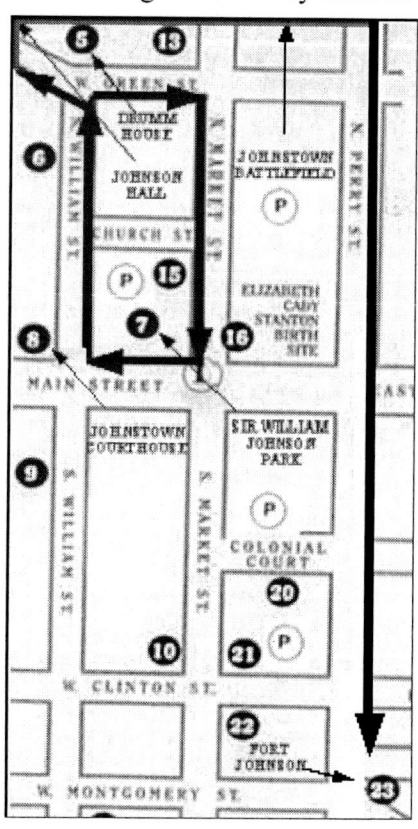

Raiders would return one more time in October of 1781 and be challenged by American forces at the Battle of Johnstown, one of the last battles of the Revolutionary War. The battlefield is an upcoming site on a recommended tour of Johnstown that follows. The first site is the Johnstown Courthouse.

Johnstown Courthouse — The courthouse can be found at the corner of West Main Street and North Williams Street. Prior to the Revolutionary War, the courthouse served Johnson's Colonial empire, the great County of Tryon. The cornerstone was laid in 1772 with the "attendance of British officers and soldiers," which "gave dignity ... to the event, while over all the group, asserting the power of the Crown, waved the broad folds of the British Flag." It is clear from this description, that, Johnstown was severely split by the Revolution.

Today the courthouse serves as the Fulton County Courthouse.

Fulton County Courthouse 1772

It is the only Colonial courthouse still in use in New York State. Bricks used to build the courthouse were shipped from England, arrived by boat in Albany and traveled to Johnstown by wagon. The first court general sessions, Tryon County, September 8, 1772. Aaron Burr tried a case here in 1812.

(Johnstown Marker)

The Drumm House — 1763

This is the oldest dwelling in Johnstown. The only survivor of six similar structures built by Sir William for his staff. Here lived Edward Wall, schoolmaster of the first free school in the colony of New York.

(Johnstown Marker)

The Drumm House — This old home can be reached by walking north on North Williams Street. On the way, you will pass the Johnstown Historical Society on the left. The society houses a museum with many historical relics from Johnstown's past.

Colonial Cemetery

Many notables of Colonial and Revolutionary days are buried here, including Colonel James Livingston and Washington Irving's sister. The unmarked grave of the last person legally hanged in Fulton County is in this cemetery.

(Johnstown Marker)

> To the memory of our historic dead who bore arms in the War of Independence and who were ever the brave defenders of the Mohawk Valley and to the early inhabitants of our city who laid here foundations so enduring.
>
> This arch is erected and dedicated by the Johnstown Chapter Daughters of the American Revolution.
>
> (Johnstown Marker)

The Drumm House is at the end of North William Street. Built in 1763 by Sir William Johnson, it is the oldest dwelling in Johnstown. It was the home of Edward Wall, schoolmaster of the first free school in New York.

Sir William Johnson Park — The park can be reached by walking east on West Green Street and

> ### Lest We Forget
>
> Commemorating the first veterans of our nation who fell in the Battle of Johnstown.
>
> One of the last battles of the American Revolution, October 25, 1781.
>
> Erected by the Fulton County Veterans Council in conjunction with the Fulton County Bicentennial Commission in the year 1976.
>
>
>
> (Johnstown Marker)

> **North, Site of
> First St. John's Church (1760)**
>
> Erected St. John's Church (1760) erected by Sir William Johnson. First church of England north of the Mohawk River.
>
> State Education Department 1940
>
> (Johnstown Marker)

turning right at North Market Street. On the way, you will pass the Colonial Cemetery on the left. Many Revolutionary War soldiers are buried here.

On North Market Street, you will pass St. John's Episcopal Church. Sir William Johnson sponsored the

> In memory of Sir William Johnson, Baronet. A man of strong character, a colossal pioneer. One of the greatest men of his time. Sole superintendent and faithful friend of the Six Nations and their Allies. Their Warragiyagey. Founder of Johnstown. He established here the first free school in the state. Born in Ireland, 1715. Died in Johnstown, 1774.
>
>
>
> Erected by the Aldine Society of Johnstown, New York. 1904.
>
> (Johnstown Marker)

Superintendent of Indian Affairs

Gaining considerable knowledge of Indian affairs, his area of responsibility for administration reached from Hudson's Bay Canada, to the Carolinas, from the Atlantic to as far west as any Indians were known.

Appointed to deal with Indians, and because of just and honest treatment of them, his influence of Indian power was tremendously important to colonial governors and their colonies.

He effected the surrender of Pontiac, at Oswego in 1766, thereby ending the Pontiac conspiracy. Moving to Johnson Hall at Johnstown, NY in 1769 his fourth and last home, he conducted very important councils with many Indians who came to speak to him, at times numbering 1000 individuals.

Here, he died, on Sunday, 11 July 1774, after holding an important Indian council. He died as he had lived, admired and trusted by the Indians, respected by the military and civil officers of the colonies, and a great credit to the public trust reposed in him.

(Johnson Hall Marker)

construction of the original church on this site. Johnson's burial site, which was once inside the old church, is now outside the current structure in Sir William Johnson Park. Also in the park is a monument placed by the Fulton County Veterans Council noting the Battle of Johnstown as one of the last battles of the Revolutionary War.

Besides Sir William Johnson, Johnstown is also noted for another of its past citizens. Across from Sir William Johnson Park on North Market Street is the site of the birthplace and home of Elizabeth Cady Stanton. She made full women's suffrage her call for liberty.

Johnson Hall — After returning to your car, the palatial Johnson home can be reached by following Route 29 north on North William Street and onto West State Street. It was from this home that Sir William Johnson presided over his Mohawk Valley empire. During the council, he made it clear that he was

Sir William Johnson presenting medals to the Indian Chiefs of the Six Nations at Johnstown, New York, 1772. Painting by Edward Lamson Henry, 1903.

(Johnson Hall Display)

opposed to the movement toward revolution. After his death, his son and the Six Nations carried forward his legacy throughout the war.

Battle of Johnstown — The battlefield is off Johnson Avenue, which is on the north side of Johnson Hall, opposite the entrance. It can be reached by returning to West State Street, continuing past the Sir William Johnson statue, turning right on Johnson Avenue and continuing past Johnson Hall to the stop sign at the intersection with O'Neil Avenue although it may be hard to find a street sign to confirm this.

On the way, you will pass a battlefield marker on the right. There is another marker near the intersection with Johnson and O'Neil Avenues.

The battlefield marks the end of an October 1781 raid through parts of the Mohawk Valley by British forces composed of Indians, Tories and British troops led by Major Ross and Captain Butler. After raiding areas to

---

Historic Battlefield — 1781

The Battle of Johnstown was fought October 25, 1781. American forces were led by Colonel Willett. The British forces were under Major Ross and Captain Butler. This site commemorates the last battle of the Revolutionary War — fought six days after General Cornwallis surrendered to General George Washington at Yorktown.

(Johnstown Marker)

the east and south of Johnstown, the British forces were attacked by American forces led by Colonel Marinus Willett. Willett divided his forces and approached the British forces from the front and rear. The frontal attack was first repulsed, but the rear force held, and after reorganizing, a second frontal attack forced the British into retreat. The American forces pursued the retreating British and they were able to overtake and rout them.

The battle was an American victory and was fought six days after the victory at Yorktown. The Battle of Johnstown was one of the last battles of the Revolutionary War.

This tablet marks the site of the battle fought in the war of the American Revolution, October 25, 1781, and was erected by the Johnstown Chapter DAR, August 31, 1901, charter day.

This we show to succeeding generations that we honor our heroic dead.

(Johnstown Marker)

Fort Johnstown — The fort can be reached by following O'Neil Avenue south to the stop sign at Pleasant Avenue and turning left at the traffic light on Pleasant Avenue, then right at the intersection with North Perry Street. Fort Johnstown is about a mile south on North Perry Street at the intersection with East Montgomery Street.

During the Revolution, Fort Johnstown was fortified and was a stronghold for the American patriots. It was also used as a jail for captured enemies. At the end of the Revolution, the fort was inspected by George Washington during his Mohawk Valley tour.

Fort Johnstown — 1774

The fort was built in 1774 by Sir William Johnson to fortify the village and it was used by loyalists during the Revolutionary War as an important civil and military prison. It was inspected by General George Washington in 1783.  When the cannon and balls were placed as a memorial in 1900, the cannon balls had to be welded together to prevent pranksters from rolling them down Perry Street hill.

(Johnstown Marker)

JOHNSTOWN TO SCHOHARIE

Mile Mark 159.2 — Depart Fort Johnson.

Mile Mark 159.8 — Reach a stop sign at the intersection with Route 30A. Turn right heading south.

Mile Mark 163.4 — Reach the intersection with Route 5 in the town of Fonda. Turn left and rejoin Route 5 for a short distance.

Mile Mark 163.8 — Route 30A diverts from Route 5. Turn right and detour south on Route 30A.

Mile Mark 164.1 — Cross the Mohawk River and bear right at the light and continue on Route 30A south.

Mile Mark 164.3 — Go under Interstate 90 and cross Route 5S in Fultonvillle.

Grave of William McConkey, Jan. 22, 1744 — Sept. 10, 1825, owner of a ferry on the Delaware River on which Washington crossed Dec. 25, 1776.

Grave of Samuel Tallmadge. Born Brookhaven, L. I., Nov. 23, 1755 — Died Apr. 1, 1825, lieutenant and adjutant in American Revolution.

State Education Department 1932

(Route 30A Markers)

Mile Mark 168.4 — Reach the junction with Route 161 in the town of Glen. Continue south on Route 30A.

Mile Mark 172.3 — On the right are the gravesites of William McConkey, who helped Washington cross the Delaware, and Samuel Tallmadge, who was a Revolutionary War adjutant.

Mile Mark 172.9 — The road splits. Bear left on Route 30A.

Mile Mark 174.5 — Pass an old Indian Trail and marker on the right.

Mile Mark 176.7 — As you come over a hill, look for the Catskill Mountains in the distance. Behind you are the Adirondack Mountains.

Mile Mark 178.2 — Reach a stop sign at the intersection with Route 162. Turn left and continue south on Route 30A.

Warrior Trail

Early Indian trail from the Mohawk south to the coast ran along Waite Drive. Used by Johnson's Raiders in 1780. Retraced by B. and D. O'Neill.

(Route 30A Marker)

Mile Mark 179.0 — Reach the intersection with US Route 20, the Cherry Valley Turnpike. About 25 miles to the west is the town of Cherry Valley. On November 11, 1778, Captain Walter Butler and two Tory companies (the same Captain Butler that was one of the leaders of the British forces at the Battle of Johnstown) along with Joseph Brant and 500 Indians attacked the town. Many villagers, including women and children, couldn't make it to the Cherry Valley fort. Although the fort held, the town was destroyed and about 50 villagers were killed and scalped by the Indians.

Further west is Cobleskill. On June 1, 1778, Joseph Brant led a raid on the town and drove off the defending Continental troops, killing Captain William Patrick, their commanding officer. The Indians then massacred many of the town's settlers.

The Cherry Hill and Cobleskill Massacres helped to provoke Washington to order Generals Clinton and Sullivan on their expedition of 1779. Clinton's campaign started at Canajoharie, a previous site on this road trip.

Mile Mark 182.9 — Reach the intersection with Route 7 at Central Bridge. Turn left and continue south on Route 30A.

Mile Mark 183.7 — Watch for a marker on the left for the site of a 1781 blockhouse.

Site of blockhouse built 1781 used by inhabitants during Indian raids.

State Education Department 1932

(Route 30A Marker)

> Site of home of Johannes Ball occupied by continental soldiers during Revolution until completion of Old Stone Fort.
>
> Schoharie County Bicentennial 1995.
>
> (Route 30 Marker)

Mile Mark 184.0 — Reach an intersection, turn right and continue south on Route 30A.

Mile Mark 184.3 — Cross over Interstate 88.

Mile Mark 185.3 — Reach the end of Route 30A and the intersection with Route 30. Turn right and continue south on Route 30.

Mile Mark 186.2 — Watch for the Christian Ball marker on the right.

Mile Mark 186.3 — Just before reaching the town of Schoharie, carefully detour onto Vrooman Cross Road that bears to the left.

Mile Mark 186.5 — Watch for the George Mann Tory Tavern and marker on the left.

The tavern is appropriately named. During August of 1777, the Schoharie militia was called-up to join the forces opposing Burgoyne's invasion down the Champlain and Hudson Valleys. Captain George Mann was the leader of the militia. However, in a

> **George Mann Tory Tavern**
>
> Known in Revolutionary days as the "the brick house at the forks of the road."
>
> State Educations Department 1932
>
> (Schoharie Marker)

surprise announcement, he declared himself "a friend of King George." Mann drew some followers from his assembled troops and joined a band of loyalists gathered through the efforts of Sir John Johnson. The loyalists seized control of a good

> **Site of Major Eckerson's Mill**
>
> After Revolution home and mill of Col. Peter Vroman, Commandant of Middle Fort.
>
> Schoharie County Bicentennial 1995
>
> (Schoharie Marker)

portion of Schoharie Valley.

Today, the Tory Tavern is a popular area restaurant and is highly recommended. The wait-staff dress in period costume.

Turn right at the intersection just past the tavern and watch for a covered pedestrian bridge on the left.

Mile Mark 186.6 — Find a parking spot near the covered bridge for a visit to old Schoharie.

Stone Church Parsonage

The first home of Rev. Johannis Schuyler, pastor of the old church fortress for 31 years.

State Education Department

(Schoharie Marker)

OLD SCHOHARIE
SCHOHARIE, NEW YORK

To reach Old Schoharie, cross the covered bridge and pass many historical sites including old homes, schools and barns. West of the covered bridge is a marker on Route 30 indicating the site of Eckerson's Mill. The former Stone Church parsonage is on the left after crossing the bridge. A little further up the street is Hartman's Dorf Palatine House originally located in Middleburgh, the former site of Fort Defyance.

At the center of old Schoharie is the Old Stone Fort. The fort was among three forts erected along Schoharie Creek to protect Schoharie Valley. After George

The Hartmann's Dorf Palatine House

Circa mid 1700's, one of the oldest buildings in the county. Built soon after the palatines settled in 1712. Originally located near Middleburgh.

(Schoharie Marker)

Mann's defection in August 1777, only one of these forts, called Fort Defyance in today's Middleburgh, was able to resist the loyalist forces. One of the

The Committee of Safety ordered three forts erected along the Schoharie Creek: Upper Fort, south of the mountain known as Vroman's Nose; Middle Fort in Weiser's Dorf (now Middleburgh); and Lower (Old Stone) Fort in Fox's Dorf. Threatened by frequent Indian and Tory raids, including attacks on Cobuskill and Vroman's Land, these and later forts provided protection for civilians and bases for military operations.

An indication of the importance General Washington placed on this region is his stationing of Continental troops here in 1778. Seasoned regiments, including the 4th Pennsylvania, 5th New York, 6th Massachusetts and elements of Morgan's Rifles were troops he could ill-afford to spare from his main army. Frequent British raids, including the massive Johnson-Brant Raid of 1780, illustrate their unrelenting efforts to disrupt grain production. There operations continued into 1782 - long after General Cornwallis had surrendered the main British army at Yorktown.

(Old Stone Fort Exhibit)

**Old Stone Fort
1772
Museum Historical
Society**
(Schoharie Marker)

defenders, Colonel John Harper, was able to escape to Albany and get help.

He returned to Schoharie with the 2nd Continental Light Dragoons, a cavalry troop, under the command of a Frenchman, Captain Vernejoux. They raided Mann's Tavern and rallied the Schoharie militia. The patriots

Revolutionary War Fort

In 1777, the pews were removed from the church, a stockade wall was erected, and the church became known as the Lower Fort. The fort was attacked once in 1780. The stockade was taken down in 1785 and the building reverted to a house of worship.

In 1844, the Schoharie congregation moved their meeting place to the newly constructed brick church in the village, and the Stone Church was used for Sunday school and an occasional funeral until 1857 when the state bought the old church for use as an armory.

(Old Stone Fort Exhibit)

Colonel John Harper

Born Boston, Mass. 1734 - Died Harpersfield, NY 1811. Frontiersman, soldier and patriot. Protector of the frontiers during the Revolution. Commandant of Schoharie Fort, 1777. Captain Rangers July 17, 1777. Guide of Gen. James Clinton on Western Expedition, 1779. Colonel of 5th Tryon County Regiment, March 3, 1780. Commandant of 2nd Regiment of Levies, May 11, 1780. Escaping vigilance of Seth's Henry Aug. 2, 1777, he escorted squadron of light horse from Albany to Schoharie where the Tory Captain McDonell was routed Aug. 3, 1777 during the Battle of Flockey.

Erected by Mr. Perry E. Taylor, Schoharie County and the State of New York, 1828.

(Schoharie Marker)

with the cavalry at the lead attacked the loyalist bands at the Battle of Flockey and returned Schoharie valley to Patriot control. The cavalry charge is said to be the first of the Revolutionary War.

Chests 1770, Painted Wood

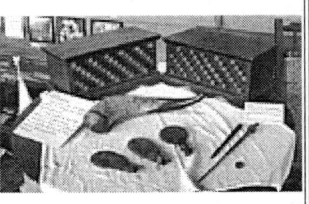

These colorful chests are wonderful examples of decorative and functional Palatine German folk art.

The chests belonged to twin sisters Margreda and Elizabeth Kniskern. The young girls took refuge in the Fort during the Johnson-Brant raid while their father, Johannes, helped to defend the Fort.

(Old Stone Fort Exhibit)

Memorial to David Ellerson
1749 - 1838

Schoharie County Revolutionary hero. Patriot soldier scout. Member of Morgan's Rifle Corps. Served at Trenton, Monmouth, Saratoga and in Sullivan's Campaign. Especially distinguished for bravery on scout duty in Schoharie Valley. Fought at Battle of Middle Fort against Col. Johnson and Chief Brant.

(Schoharie Marker)

The War for Independence
A Forgotten Frontier

The fertile soil and innovative agricultural techniques for growing grain had made the Schoharie Valley prosperous. Its hardworking farmers produced enough grain to feed its civilians and send the surplus to American troops. Hence, the valley's wheat production became a target for disruption by the British during the Revolutionary War.

With many Loyalists (Tories) and Native Americans of mixed allegiance in the valley, suspicions ran high and even families were split. The local Committee of Safety was active in identifying Loyalists, imprisoning them or forcing them to relocate. A Tory uprising paralyzed the valley during the Burgoyne campaign in 1777. It was put down by a troop of Continental cavalry at the Battle of the Flockey, the US Army's first cavalry charge.

(Old Stone Fort Exhibit)

> **Above**
>
> Cannon Ball Hole made when the Fort was attacked by the British Tories and Indians under Sir John Johnson and the Indian Chief Joseph Brant during the raid of 1780.
>
> (Schoharie Marker)

The loyalists, however, would return to Schoharie many times during the war. They would destroy precious grain crops and try to reclaim property and family left behind. Schoharie was also attacked during the Great Raid of 1780. The Second Regiment from nearby Schenectady, the final site on this road trip, helped to garrison the forts on the Schoharie River during the Great Raid.

Major Melanchthon Woolsey commanded the garrison of about 200. Sir John Johnson's forces greatly outnumbered the patriots about 7 to 1. However, the accuracy of the fire by the sharpshooters in the tower of the Old Stone Fort repulsed Johnson's raiders. When he turned a swivel gun on the fort, Woolsey attempted to surrender, but when he sent the surrender flag out, it was reportedly shot down by Timothy Murphy, a sharpshooter in the tower. Woolsey ordered Murphy's arrest, but mutiny in the ranks prevented the action. In the meantime, Johnson decided the fort was too strong and retreated.

Timothy Murphy

Timothy Murphy is the folk hero of the Schoharie Valley. The dark eyed, light-hearted Irishman has been described as quick-witted and short with a muscular frame. He was born in Minisink, New Jersey in 1751 and first enlisted for military service in 1775.

Murphy was noted for his marksmanship and has been credited with killing General Fraser at Saratoga in 1777. By 1778, Murphy had earned respect as a scout in the Schoharie and Mohawk Valleys and in 1770 enrolled in the 15th Regiment of Albany County Militia that was stationed in the Schoharie forts. He is credited with risking his life and saving the Middle Fort through acts of insubordination.

(Old Stone Fort Exhibit)

Today, the Old Stone Fort is a museum with many exhibits and displays. The museum is open May through October from 10 AM to 5 PM, Tuesdays through Saturdays; open Sundays from noon to 5PM; open Mondays in July, August, holidays from 10 AM to 5 PM.

Schoharie

Also called Fountaintown. Original villages of Brunnen Dorf, Smith's Dorf, Fox Dorf.

Schoharie County Bicentennial 1995

(Schoharie Marker)

Site of First School

In Schoharie Village, built about 1740.

State Education Department

(Schoharie Marker)

Site of First Parsonage of P. N. Sommer, Lutheran Parson

Erected in 1743.

Present building has been preserved by St. Paul's Lutheran Church at Schoharie.

Oldest Building

In Schoharie County 1743 Lutheran Parsonage, Peter N. Sommers, Dominie, first services held Sept. 12, 1743.

State Education Department 1935

(Schoharie Markers)

SCHOHARIE TO SCHENECTADY

Mile Mark 186.6 — Return to your car across the covered bridge. If time permits, go a little further south on Route 30 and visit downtown Schoharie. There are several historic markers to see as well as the Old Palentine House, which is about a half mile east of the downtown area.

From Schoharie, reverse direction on Route 30 heading north.

Mile Mark 188.1 — Reach the intersection with Route 30A. Bear right and continue on Route 30 North.

Mile Mark 189.9 — Go over Interstate 88 and reach a stop sign at the intersection with Route 7. Turn right heading east on Route 7.

Mile Mark 194.9 — Reach the intersection with Route 395 in Quaker Street. Bear left and continue going east on Route 7.

Mile Mark 198.2 — Reach the center of Duanesburg and the intersection with US Route 20. Continue going straight on Route 7 East.

Mile Mark 203.0 — Go under Interstate 88.

Mile Mark 204.9 — Go over Interstate 90 (for the last time).

Mile Mark 206.7 — Creep to the intersection with Broadway and Route 7. Depart Route 7, which goes left, and continue going straight on Broadway into the city of Schenectady.

Mile Mark 208.7 — As you approach Interstate 890, get into the middle lane and go under the interstate.

Mile Mark 208.9 — Reach a split in the road. Get into the middle lane and continue going straight on Broadway.

Mile Mark 209.3 — Reach downtown Schenectady. Watch for the intersection with State Street and Route 5. Turn left and rejoin Route 5 heading west.

Mile Mark 209.8 — Watch for walking bridge that crosses Route 5 at Schenectady Community College. Turn right just before the walking bridge on Washington Street, although you may find it difficult to find a street sign identifying the street. Find a parking place for a visit to the Schenectady Stockade.

Arrive in the Schenectady Stockade.

SCHENECTADY STOCKADE
SCHENECTADY, NEW YORK

When the Revolution broke out Schenectady was already an old American city — over 110 years old.

It had survived the Schenectady Massacre of 1690 and had become an important river port on the Mohawk River as well as an industrious town on the Albany Road.

In 1775, a Committee of Safety and Correspondence was formed and troops were raised for the defense of Fort Ticonderoga. The Schenectady and Albany committees frequently cooperated with the Tryon County Committee. Later, when the Continental Line was organized, the men from Schenectady who enlisted for the Revolutionary War were assigned to the First New York Line, Colonel Van Schaick's regiment.

The town was fortified and garrisoned during the war. There was a stockade enclosing the village with blockhouses at the angles, and there was a fort at the junction of Ferry and Front streets. The General Hospital for the Northern District and barracks for the troops were each located east of the stockade on Union Street near today's Union College. Vast numbers of American soldiers, who were wounded in valley conflicts, were brought to Schenectady by river for treatment.

Schenectady was a haven of refuge during the Revolution for the people of the Mohawk Valley fleeing from British-Indian raids along the river. It was also the starting point for several American military expeditions. The most important was General Clinton's expedition against the Indians, which left Schenectady for Canajoharie in May of 1779.

Just to the west of where you are standing lies the traditional homeland of the Mohawk people. Mohawk villages once dotted the landscape near the river that bears their name, sustained by the region's abundant fish, wildlife, and fertile farmland. The river provided the Mohawk people easy access to other Iroquois nations to the west and to European trading posts at Schenectady and Albany to the east.

The Dutch were the first Europeans to settle in the Mohawk Valley, establishing a farming and fur trading community at Schenectady in 1661. The Dutch brought to the area the first African slaves, who were used as farmhands, servants and even soldiers. German, British, and other settlers came into the region in the early 1700s, establishing a dozen settlements upriver within a half-century.

Mohawk Valley residents—Native, African, and European alike—suffered greatly during colonial struggles between England and France. New York, a British colony since 1554, was invaded numerous times by French forces from Canada. Villages of the Mohawk people, who were allies of the British, were destroyed in 1666 and 1693, and the European settlement at Schenectady was burned in 1690. During the American Revolution (1775-1783), the region was again at the center of intense frontier fighting. Many communities were destroyed as the British and Americans, along with numerous Indian allies, fought to control the strategic Mohawk Valley transportation route.

(New York Thruway Marker)

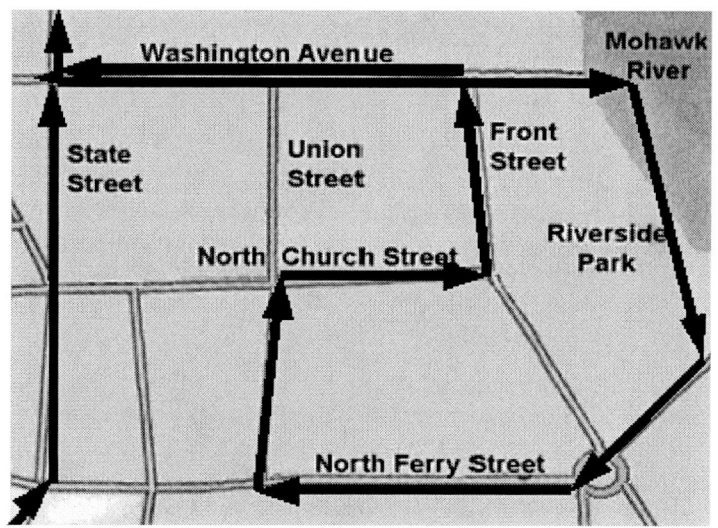

John Glen House — Begin a walking tour of the Schenectady Stockade at the John Glen House, 59 Washington Street. George Washington was entertained and lodged here in 1775. He occupied the bedroom on the second floor to the right of the front of the building. Washington visited Schenectady several time during the Revolution, each time to inspect Schenectady's fortifications.

John Glen House 1740

Washington occupied N. E. bedroom, second floor on first visit to Schenectady in 1775.

State Education Department 1932

(Schenectady Stockade Marker)

> **Robert Sanders House
> 1750**
>
> Washington visited here in 1775. Later became Schenectady Female Academy.
>
> State Education Department 1932
>
> (Schenectady Stockade Marker)

Robert Sanders House — Across the street from the Glen House is the Robert Sanders House at 43 Washington Avenue. Washington also visited this home in 1775 for tea. The house was built in 1750.

Schenectady Historical Society — Just up the street past the YMCA is the Schenectady Historical Society at 32 Washington Street. The society houses collections from the colonial periods including the

> **Circa 1786**
>
> John Baptist Van Epps was a fur trader and also operated a fleet of boats. At this site he ran the ferry dock at which, George Washington landed on one of his visits to Schenectady.
>
> (Schenectady Marker)

Revolutionary War. The "Sons of Liberty" flag carried by the First Line of New York during the war can be found among the collections.

Riverside Park — At the end of Washington Street is Riverside Park. Historically, this area was the beginning of navigation on the Mohawk River. Soldiers, settlers and traders headed west from the port that once thrived here. Boat builders made river bateaux, and warehouses lined the riverbank filled with grain, salt, potash, furs and other goods that were loaded and

> ### Site of "Queen's Fort"
>
> Built in 1705, as a temple stockade. Rebuilt in 1735, of heavy hewn timbers set on a stonewall ten feet high. Fort was one hundred feet square, with blockhouse at each corner, twenty-four feet square and twenty feet high. Was capable of holding three hundred men.
>
>
>
> Entered by a large swinging gate, raised like a drawbridge. Six cannon commanded the approaches from all sides. Open square within, was used as a parade and drill ground.
>
> Taken down during the Revolution, the timbers were used to frame the soldier's barrack, at the corner of Union and Lafayette Streets.
>
> Tablet erected by Common Council on Centennial Anniversary of Incorporation of City, March 26, 1898.
>
> (Schenectady Marker)

unloaded from these boats. Ferrys moved back and forth across the river.

As noted by a marker near the park, one soldier that landed at the port was George Washington. The port was a part of one of his inspection tours during the Revolutionary War.

> Circa 1748-1785, House of Colonel Christopher Yates, leader of the Sons of Liberty, chairman of the Committee of Safety, ca.1771-1776.
>
> (Schenectady Stockade Marker)

A cannon in the park near North Ferry Street reminds us that the river formed a geographic barrier that helped to protect Schenectady from attack during the war.

Colonel Christopher Yates House — The home can be found near the rotary at the intersection of Front and North Ferry Streets. In the center of the rotary is the statue of Lawrence the Indian and a marker for Queen's Fort.

The Colonel Christopher Yates house is near the rotary at 30 Front Street. Yates served in the New York Militia during the Revolutionary War. His son, Joseph C. Yates, was governor of New York in 1823.

St. George's Episcopal Church — The church is located just south of the rotary on North Ferry Street. The congregation was first organized in 1735. The foundation for the present church was laid in 1759 and completed in 1762. Its construction was, in great part, financially supported by Sir William Johnson, who was given his own pew for his own use. The church is among the oldest in the state. During the Revolution, the building was used for a period as a barracks for Continental Troops.

Northeast Corner of Stockade

Is marked by this tablet. A blockhouse, with garrison and cannon stood in the angle of stockade, facing the ferry, at foot of this street. North line of stockade extended from this tablet direct to the riverbank near intersection of Front Street and Washington Avenue.

Saint George's Church

First service of the Episcopal Church in Schenectady was held by Rev. John Miller, in 1695. Erection of present church edifice was begun in 1759, and was several years in building. First Resident Clergyman was Rev. William Andrews, 1773. Sir William Johnson was a frequent worshiper here and contributed liberally to its erection and support. The tower, originally of wood, was rebuilt of stone in 1870.

Schenectady Centennial Tablet, March 26, 1898.

Replaced 1936, Nathaniel Spalding, City Historian.

(Schenectady Stockade Markers)

Yates House — The home, which is classic Dutch architecture, is just around the corner on the north side of Union Street. As noted by the marker, it is one of the oldest homes in the stockade.

Yates House

Reputed oldest house in city. Typical early 18th century home of Abraham Yates

State Education Department 1932

(Schenectady Stockade Marker)

Dutch Church — The church is at the corner of North Church and Union Streets. It is home to the oldest congregation of the Stockade, ca. 1680.

Second Site of Dutch Church

This was at intersection of Union and Church Streets built 1734. Taken down and rebuilt on present site 1814. Burned 1861 and rebuilt 1863. East corner of these streets, eight persons were killed, and on south west near Washington Avenue on north side of Union Street, two were killed and seven taken prisoners.

(Schenectady Stockade Marker)

First proprietors of Schenectady. By purchase from Dutch West India Company.

Arendt Van Curler
Bastian De Winter
Philip Hendrickse Brouwer
Sander Leendertse Glen
Symon Volkertse Veeder
Pieter Adriaense Van Wogulum
Tuenise Cornelisse Swart
Marten Cornelisse Van Esselstey
William Teller
Garrit Bancker
Arendt Andriesse Bratt
Pieter Jacobse Borsboom
Pieter Danielse Van Olinda
Jan Barentse Wemple
Jacques Cornelisse Van Slyck

Centennial Anniversary Tablet, March 26, 1898

(Schenectady Stockade Marker)

Rosa House — At 14 North Church Street, the house is also one of the oldest in the stockade. As indicated by the marker, it was built before 1700.

Oldest House in City

Built before 1700 by Hendrick Brouwer a fur trader, who died here 1707. Sold 1799 to James Rosa, Supt. Mohawk & Hudson R.R. 1831.

(Schenectady Marker)

Cur Non!

On June 11, 1825, Major General Marquis de Lafayette, soldier, statesman, citizen of France and of the United States, was the guest of the Honorable Joseph C. Yates, Governor of the State of New York.

Erected by the American Friends of Lafayette, May 20, 1961.

(Schenectady Stockade Marker)

Governor Yates House — Near the intersection of North Church and Front Streets is the Governor Yates house. Joseph Yates, son of Colonel Christopher Yates, was the first mayor of Schenectady and the 4th Governor of New York. Lafayette was entertained here during one of his visits after the war in the early 1800's.

Room and Board for the Evening — There are a couple great possibilities for room and board in the Schenectady area. The stockade has a B&B on Union Street, the English Garden B&B (518-372-4390). It is about a half-block east of the intersection with Union and North Ferry Streets and is on the north side of

Union Street. A little further up Union Street is the Van Dyke (518-381-1111), a great spot for dinner and evening jazz entertainment.

Another possibility is on the north side of the Mohawk River where Continental Officers were once entertained. Today, the Glen

Gateway Landing
Schenectady Harbor 1660-1820

Head of navigation on the Mohawk, this thriving gateway port funneled traders, soldiers and settlers west for over 160 years. Warehouses — filled with furs, grain, salt, potash and other goods — lined the far bank of the Binnekill. Hundreds of river bateaux and later Schenectady boats were made in nearby boatyards. General Philip Schuyler departed this site August 21, 1792 to survey the Mohawk. His western inland lock navigation company (1792-1820) pioneered the way for the Erie Canal. The harbor was destroyed in the great fire of 1819.

(Schenectady Marker)

Glen Sanders House

Erected in 1713, officers entertained here in Revolutionary War.

NY State Highway

(Route 5 Marker)

Sanders Mansion (518-374-7262) is still a great place for dinner and an overnight stay. The mansion is just across the river and can be reached by following Route 5 west for about a half-mile. On the way, you'll pass a Gateway Landing marker that is in a small park near the water's edge. On the marker is a depiction of Schenectady Harbor in 1814 by L. F. Tantillo. As noted by the marker in the parking lot, the base structure of the Glen Sanders House was built in 1713.

The end of the American Revolution began an exciting new chapter in the history of the Mohawk Valley. Britain had kept its colonies from expanding beyond the Appalachians, forcing a growing population to remain on overcrowded farms with failing soil and limited opportunities. Accounts from returning Revolutionary War soldiers about spectacular lands beyond the mountains inspired generations of easterners to dream of moving west. The story of the Mohawk Valley, from 1790 to 1850, is the story of thousands of people realizing this dream.

Boat passenger service began on the Mohawk in the 1790s, using lightweight bateaux and "Durham" boats built in Schenectady to navigate the narrow channels and rapids upriver. After 1800, turnpikes competed with the river route for customers, and both became important for moving soldiers and supplies to the Lake Ontario/Lake Erie frontier during the War of 1812.

The Erie Canal, completed in 1825, greatly increased the number of people traveling through the Mohawk Valley. For decades, canal packet boats—each carrying up to one hundred passengers—moved day and night through this area, the first leg of their 363-mile trip to the canal's end at Buffalo. Although most westbound passenger traffic switched to faster railroad service in the 1840s, the Erie Canal remained a vital link in developing the Mohawk Valley's economy throughout the nineteenth century. Many scenic sections of the Erie Canal can be seen from the Thruway today.

(New York Thruway Marker)

BIBLIOGRAPHY

Bobrick, Benson, **Angel in the Whirlwind,** Penguin Books, New York, 1997.

Colbrath, William, **Days of Siege: A Journal of the Siege of Fort Stanwix in 1777,** Edited by Larry Lowenthal, Eastern National Park & Monument Association, 1995.

Greene, Nelson, **The Old Mohawk Turnpike**, Nelson Greene, Fort Plain, New York, 1924.

National Park Service, U.S. Department of the Interior, **Fort Stanwix, National Monument, New York,** GPO:2002-491-282/40261.

New York State Office of Parks, Recreation and Historic Preservation, **Fort Ontario, State Historic Site, Oswego, New York**, 2000.

New York State Office of Parks, Recreation and Historic Preservation, **Herkimer Home State Historic Site**, March 2001.

New York State Office of Parks, Recreation and Historic Preservation, **Oriskany Battlefield Walking Tour**, July 1999.

New York State Office of Parks, Recreation and Historic Preservation, **Oriskany Battlefield, State Historic Site, Oriskany, New York**, March 2002.

Old Stone Fort Museum Complex, **The Battle of the Flockey,** The Troy Savings Bank Charitable Foundation, 2002.

Purcell, L. Edward and David F. Burg, Editors, **The World Almanac of the American Revolution**, Pharos Books, New York, 1992.

Schenectady Heritage Area Visitor Center, **Schenectady Self-Guided Stockade Walking Tour,** 2004.

Stember, Sol, **The Bicentennial Guide to the American Revolution: The War in the North, Volume One,** E. P. Dutton & Co., Inc., New York, 1974.

Raymond C. Houghton is a freelance historian and sole proprietor of Cyber Haus of Delmar, NY. He is a retired college professor, former government bureaucrat, Vietnam Veteran and one-time, General Electric employee. He has honors from the Department of Commerce, is listed in Who's Who in America, and holds a doctorate from Duke University.